Wizards, Wardrobes and Wookiees

Navigating Good and Evil in Harry Potter, Narnia and Star Wars

Connie Neal

IVP Books

An imprint of InterVarsity Press
Downers Grove, Illinois

InterVarsity Press
P.O. Box 1400, Downers Grove, IL 60515-1426
World Wide Web: www.ivpress.com
E-mail: email@ivpress.com

InterVarsity Press® is the book-publishing division of InterVarsity Christian Fellowship/USA®, a student movement active on campus at hundreds of universities, colleges and schools of nursing in the United States of America, and a member movement of the International Fellowship of Evangelical Students. For information about local and regional activities, write Public Relations Dept., InterVarsity Christian Fellowship/USA, 6400 Schroeder Rd., P.O. Box 7895, Madison, WI 53707-7895, or visit the IVCF website at <www.intervarsity.org>.

All Scripture quotations, unless otherwise indicated, are taken from the Holy Bible, New International Version®. NIV®. Copyright ©1973, 1978, 1984 by International Bible Society. Used by permission of Zondervan Publishing House. All rights reserved.

Design: Cindy Kiple
Images: dark sky: Aleruaro/Getty Images
        door knob: Clayton Hansen/istockphoto

ISBN 978-0-8308-3366-5

Printed in the United States of America ∞

Library of Congress Cataloging-in-Publication Data

Neal, C. W. (Connie W.) 1958-
    Wizards, wardrobes & wookiees: navigating good and evil in Harry
Potter, Star Wars & the Chronicles of Narnia/Connie Neal.
        p. cm.
    Includes bibliographical references.
    ISBN 978-0-8308-3366-5 (pbk.: alk. paper)
    1. Spiritual warfare. 2. Good and evil. 3. Heroes. 4. Potter,
Harry (Fictitious character) 5. Lewis, C. S. (Clive Staples),
1898-1963. Chronicles of Narnia. 6. Star Wars films. I. Title.
    BV4509.5.N42 2007
    261.5'7—dc22
                                                              2007004008

P	18	17	16	15	14	13	12	11	10	9	8	7	6	5	4	3	2	1
Y	22	21	20	19	18	17	16	15	14	13	12	11	10	09	08	07		

Contents

Featured Series

Harry Potter, by J. K. Rowling

Harry Potter and the Sorcerer's Stone. New York: Arthur A. Levine, 1997.

Harry Potter and the Chamber of Secrets. New York: Arthur A. Levine, 1999.

Harry Potter and the Prisoner of Azkaban. New York: Arthur A. Levine, 1999.

Harry Potter and the Goblet of Fire. New York: Arthur A. Levine, 2000.

Harry Potter and the Order of the Phoenix. New York: Arthur A. Levine, 2003.

Harry Potter and the Half-Blood Prince. New York: Arthur A. Levine, 2005.

The Chronicles of Narnia, by C. S. Lewis

The Magician's Nephew. New York: Collier, 1955.

The Lion, the Witch and the Wardrobe. New York: Macmillan, 1950.

Prince Caspian. New York: Macmillan, 1951.

The Voyage of the "Dawn Treader." New York: Macmillan, 1952.

The Silver Chair. New York: Macmillan, 1953.

The Horse and His Boy. New York: Macmillan, 1954.

The Last Battle. New York: Macmillan, 1956.

Star Wars, directed by George Lucas

The Phantom Menace. Twentieth Century Fox, 1999.

Attack of the Clones. Twentieth Century Fox, 2002.

Revenge of the Sith. Twentieth Century Fox, 2005.

A New Hope. Twentieth Century Fox, 1977.

The Empire Strikes Back. Twentieth Century Fox, 1980.

Return of the Jedi. Twentieth Century Fox, 1983.

Acknowledgments

Writing this book became an interesting journey in itself! Along that road I had to rely on the help of my own "hero team," who offered direction, suggestions, editorial support, valuable knowledge (especially from my *Star Wars* mentor, Josh Lickter) and encouragement. The following thanks are due.

Thanks to my daughter, Casey, whose understanding of classic story structure and insistence that I read *The Writer's Journey* by Christopher Vogler presented the framework I was looking for to offer the structure to frame this book.

Thanks to my son, Taylor, who has been a card-carrying Jedi Knight since his eighth birthday (nine years ago). His protective oversight of all things related to *Star Wars* helped me learn to love the series and make sense of it in this context.

Special thanks are due to Pastor Josh Lickter who acted as my *Star Wars* mentor and guide. Where I lacked intricate knowledge of *Star Wars*, he has devoted himself to this study. He was gracious enough to read the manuscript, catch and correct any errors related to *Star Wars*, while also suggesting spiritual themes I might pursue. Dick Staub's book *Christian Wisdom of the Jedi Masters* was helpful as I sought to grasp the spiritual themes in *Star Wars*. The works of Joseph Campbell provided one view of mythic stories that prodded me to develop my own without giving up a distinctly Christian perspective.

I am ever grateful to the Lord, and to my husband, Patrick; their constant support makes it possible for me to keep writing. My friend Kim covers me in prayer, which makes a tremendous difference. Toward the end of this book Sherrie Lorance came alongside to review the manuscript and offer encouragement.

Thanks are due to the editorial and marketing team at InterVarsity Press: Cindy Bunch, who dared to envision such a book; Dave Zimmerman, who worked on content editing; Cindy Kiple, who created such a beautiful cover; and all the others on the IVP hero team who worked toward creating this book and delivering it to the readers.

Although it might go without saying, it should be clearly stated that I am dearly grateful to J. K. Rowling for creating the Harry Potter series, C. S. Lewis for creating The Chronicles of Narnia and George Lucas for creating the *Star Wars* movies. These stories have been priceless in enriching my life and my children's childhood (not to mention Taylor's eighth birthday party, which was the greatest *Star Wars* party in the galaxy!).

Lastly, I am grateful to you the reader and thinker who will take this book, read it, reflect on it and hopefully discuss it with others who love these stories as you do.

Introduction

The Hero's Journey, Mythic Archetypes and Biblical Insights

"The heroes of all time have gone before us."

Joseph Campbell

What is it about *Star Wars* that has generation after generation devoted to this cosmic battle between good and evil? What causes devotees—especially younger ones—to cluster excitedly together with their X-wing starfighters, intently playing out the exploits of Luke Skywalker and Han Solo for hours on end, reenacting scenes, debating strategy, rehearsing the story over and over and over? What is it about this story that has such power to captivate us—not only children, but people of all ages?

What has made hundreds of millions of us—from diverse cultures all around the earth and speaking at least sixty-two different languages—love the Harry Potter stories, even if warned to avoid them like the devil himself? What has elementary school children reading and rereading the Harry Potter books, some almost as long as the Bible (longer if you consider them combined)?

What makes the Chronicles of Narnia, a children's series of fantasy stories, the most popular works of an Oxford professor, medieval scholar and eminent theologian more than forty years after his death?

Whatever *it* is, it made the movie versions of *Star Wars: The Revenge of the Sith*, *Harry Potter and the Goblet of Fire*, and *The Chronicles of Narnia: The Lion, the Witch and the Wardrobe* the top three money-making films of 2005. There must be some common denominator that explains this almost irresistible attraction people have—regardless of age or culture—for such fantastic stories. What do such stories have in common that deeply satisfies the longings of the human heart, soul and mind? I believe it has something to do with how these stories all engage in a classic battle between good and evil. It also has to do with the power of myth—repeated archetypes crafted by the human imagination for generations into fantastic stories of heroic journeys.

WHAT ARE FANTASTIC STORIES?

Some of the most powerful literature is made up of fantastic stories—fairy tales, fantasy fiction, folklore and myths. These kinds of stories take us beyond the limitations of our own world through some mode of the supernatural. Looking back on myth and classic literature in every culture, scholars have identified story patterns, themes and mythic archetypes (standard character-types such as the hero, the mentor and the villain) that show up consistently in stories passed on from generation to generation. The basic story line shared by such stories has come to be known popularly as "the hero's journey," chronicling unlikely heroes who grow to confront evil and overcome evil with good. You can readily find this pattern in *Star Wars*, the Chronicles of Narnia and the Harry Potter series.

Fantastic stories take the audience along the path of the hero—who can be male or female—throughout the journey in his or her quest. The hero's journey has been recognized as having so much power to entertain and satisfy audiences that it has become standard training for screenwriters. Christopher Vogler, a former story-crafter for Disney Animation, showed writers how to incorporate these classic patterns and character types—not as a rigid grid simply to be filled in by a storyteller but as a flexible guide for storytelling. Here is his summary as it appears in his book *The Writer's Journey*:

1. HEROES are introduced in the ORDINARY WORLD, where
2. They receive the CALL TO ADVENTURE.
3. They are RELUCTANT at first or REFUSE THE CALL, but
4. are encouraged by a MENTOR to
5. CROSS THE FIRST THRESHOLD and enter the Special World where
6. They encounter TESTS, ALLIES, and ENEMIES.
7. They APPROACH THE INMOST CAVE, crossing a second threshold
8. where they endure the ORDEAL.
9. They take possession of their REWARD and
10. are pursued on THE ROAD BACK to the Ordinary World.
11. They cross the third threshold, experience a RESURRECTION, and are transformed by the experience.
12. They RETURN WITH THE ELIXIR, a boon or treasure to benefit the Ordinary World.[1]

Given the immense success of such a story structure throughout history and across cultures, I was left to wonder: there must be an explanation for such universal acceptance and perhaps something of great value for us. C. S. Lewis, author of the Chronicles of Narnia, saw in myth, fairy-tales and most fantastic stories "a real though unfocused gleam of divine truth falling on human imagination."[2] Might that explain the universal attraction toward such fantastic stories involving the battle between good and evil? Might the Great Storyteller, in creating humanity in his image, have imprinted our imaginations with his favorite story line, one to satisfy the longings he put within our hearts and minds when he made us? Might such stories—which most of us already know—be useful in preparing us and our children for the battles between good and evil we encounter in our own lives?

In thinking along these lines, I wondered if herein might be a kernel of truth that could grow into spiritual fruit. Happily, I concluded that there is. If you enjoy any or all of these fantastic stories which are the focus of this volume, you've already made a connection with the powerful themes woven into them. This book will take you one step further into the extraordinary realm to consider and experience your part in the ongoing battle between good and evil. In case you have not read all the books in these series, I've done my best to avoid spoilers. However, you may find some plot points revealed. So be forewarned.

MYTH AND TRUTH

Because the terms *myth* and *truth* are used in various ways and hold various meanings, we need to address what a myth is and its importance for our purposes. Generally speaking, myths are stories crafted by a culture in their attempt to explain their understanding of the world, including the supernatural world of gods and monsters. Some tend to think of "myths" as stories that are too fantastic to be believable and are therefore untrue. Two acclaimed scholars and authors of fantastic fiction came to see it differently. J. R. R. Tolkien, renowned by fantasy fans for *The Hobbit* and the *Lord of the Rings* trilogy was friends with C. S. Lewis. Both being professors of literature at Oxford, and members of the literary club Inklings, their discussions often centered on literary themes. However, Tolkien also ventured to speak to Lewis—an avowed atheist at the time—about his faith in God, Jesus Christ and the Bible.

Tolkien approached the subject in an ingenious way. He started at a point of common interest, their shared love of myth and fantastic stories. By making a connection between the mythic stories they both loved and the biblical truths Tolkien sincerely believed, he was able to lead Lewis from thinking of myth as "lies though breathed through silver" to seeing them as "a real though unfocused gleam of divine truth falling on human imagination." Tolkien advanced the idea that "Since all humankind comes from God, not only abstract thought but also their imaginative invention originates in God, and reflects something of eternal truth. . . . Therefore even pagan myths cannot be totally 'lies' since they always capture something of the truth."[3]

Tolkien, seeing myth as "invention about truth" ventured further and made the connection between the mythic stories they both loved and the story of Jesus Christ in the Bible. To Tolkien "the story of Christ appears . . . as the culminating point of human history and the summit of Fairy-story." Tolkien proposed the story of Christ's incarnation, life, death and resurrection as "true myth." The story line held all the classic patterns and archetypes common in mythic tales, even the part about the dying and rising God. The essential difference was that this "myth" actually happened in human history. It was *true* myth, the fulfillment of all the longings of the human spirit reflected in mythic stories throughout history.

This shared exploration of mythology, the meaning of myth, and the *true myth* or myth that became fact played out on earth in the life, death and resurrection of Jesus, was the path that led C. S. Lewis to convert to Christianity. Eventually he was persuaded by Tolkien and concluded, "The story of Christ is simply a true myth: a myth working on us in the same way as the others, but with this tremendous difference that it *really happened:* and one must be content to accept it in the same way, remembering that it is God's myth where the others are men's myths."[4] Lewis went on to write fantasy fiction along Christian themes and become a brilliant theologian.

In agreeing with their perspective on myth and truth, I believe exploring the fantasy stories our generation loves could be spiritually provocative and instructive as we consider the conflict between good and evil.

However, I don't think ultimate truth can be found in fantastic stories apart from the Bible. Mythic tales and fantastic stories can depict the longings of the human heart, mind, soul and spirit, but they alone cannot fulfill those longings. The story can depict a triumph over evil, but we still need God's power to effect that kind of victory in real life situations. I believe we will only find fulfillment to the longings stirred up by fantasy fiction if we fully experience the life—or hero's journey—offered us in the Bible. We can only triumph over evil by the power of the Holy Spirit, experienced as we cross over into the extraordinary kind of life God wants for us.

I believe the Bible to be God's holy, final word on life and truth; but we need to go further than just believing. We must answer God's call and cross the threshold. We must allow him to transform us in the course of our own life's journey so that we can effectively join the battle and do our part to fight evil in our hearts, our minds and our world.

The purpose of this book goes beyond entertaining you or stirring up interesting thoughts, although I've tried to make it entertaining and interesting. My aim is to go beyond just thinking about these things to *experiencing* the exciting adventure God created us to experience: to actively participate in the battles against evil. I hope this book will connect the stories you know well and enjoy with biblical lessons that will empower you and transform your life to be mighty for God. I pray that you will prepare yourself fully for the ordeals we all will face, and that you will come through (with scars from battles won) to enjoy the rewards and return with the elixir of life to share with others to their benefit. The real hope of this book is that we will live powerful lives on the side of good, helping to defeat evil in our world.

WHY STAR WARS, HARRY POTTER AND THE CHRONICLES OF NARNIA?

I've chosen *Star Wars*, the Harry Potter series and the Chronicles of Narnia as stories most beloved by our generation, as evidenced by book sales and movie box office receipts. These three works of fantasy are the most popular at this time, so most likely to be familiar. I've also chosen them because all three authors were well versed in the classic story patterns and mythic archetypes that interest us here.

Did you know George Lucas followed the classic mythic structure and archetypes to create his galactic mythology in *Star Wars*? He credited this understanding to his study of Joseph Campbell's text, *The Hero with a Thousand Faces*, which codified classic mythic elements. Lucas even consulted Campbell and had him review the films to make sure his use of mythic archetypes was correct.

Did you know J. K. Rowling has a degree in the classics (and French) from Exeter University (*not* a background in the occult, as some accused her of)? Her knowledge of classic literary structure, mythic archetypes, and an integration of fairy tale, folklore, legend and fantasy can all be clearly seen in Harry Potter.

C. S. Lewis majored in philosophy, the classics and English literature at Oxford, where he also taught. So we see a common literary thread as well as a common profession of a Christian faith between Rowling and Lewis. (Contrary to what you may have heard, J. K. Rowling professes a Christian faith and belongs to the Church of Scotland, where she has had her children christened).

FEARS ABOUT READING FANTASY STORIES

Given the recent controversy surrounding Harry Potter I feel I must briefly address the selection of these works in a Christian context. Some in the Christian community have been dissecting popular fantasy fiction, to deem each particular work holy or unholy. I approach this from a different angle. The Bible forbids such practices as magic and spells, but such things can be used as a literary device without condoning such activity in our world. I look at fantasy as fantasy, myth as myth, folklore as

folklore, and fairy tales as fairy tales. I also value the fact that classic
mythic patterns and archetypes have been preserved throughout human
history. Modern writers have given them a fresh twist, but the classic patterns remain. I look at the classic patterns of fantastic stories, especially
the battle between good and evil, and find universal spiritual quests reflected there.

My biblical beliefs have not been hurt by reading fantasy, and if I
thought there was such a danger I would not encourage such reading.
Considering the battle between good and evil in such stories has given
me fresh perspective on how I fight that battle in my own life, which
is governed by the Bible. Neither has reading fantasy hurt my children's
faith in God, because I am careful to teach them the unique place of
the Bible and that all other stories are in a different category. We parents must be careful to teach our children about the Bible (and that the
fantastic stories therein, while miraculous, are true). We also need to
teach them to distinguish between fantasy, reality and that which is miraculous.

Indeed, by relating such universally enjoyed fantasy stories to the Bible we can see fresh ways to enrich our spiritual lives and better participate in our world's battles between good and evil. We can bring back
with us an expanded sense of imagination, a joy at thinking there is more
to the world than meets the eye, and a larger view of the need to fight
evil in its cosmic form. When we read fantasy stories we gain a sense that
we don't know all there is to know. This humility keeps us seeking,
which is a treasure we can bring away from such reading. We can also
find a way to connect with our culture and form common points of interest. We can share God with people as we relate God's stories to those
they already love.

Being a fan of the Great Storyteller, I appreciate the gift of imagination, and I enjoy using mine. I hope you will engage your imagination
and intellect as we explore this theory: What if this classic pattern seen

commonly in ancient stories could lead us into life-enhancing spiritual insights when aligned with biblical truths? What if focusing on the battles between good and evil in Harry Potter, the Chronicles of Narnia and *Star Wars* helps us navigate toward good and overcome evil in our world and personal lives? Consider this a call to join the spiritual battles of our day.

1

"The Hero" and Would-Be Heroes Among Us

"You . . . This isn't a criticism, Harry! But you do . . .
sort of . . . I mean—don't you think you've got a bit of
a—*saving-people-thing*?"

*Hermione to Harry, Harry Potter and the Order of the
Phoenix*

Therefore, since we are surrounded by such a great
cloud of witnesses, let us throw off everything that
hinders and the sin that so easily entangles, and let
us run with perseverance the race marked out for us.

Hebrews 12:1

Everyone loves a hero, right? And why not? Every hero has a purpose, a quest, a calling to overcome evil with good. He or she must venture into the unknown to seek that which is meant to be found. The hero must face daunting tests and trials, get past threatening monsters, unveil dangerous imposters, fight evil in various forms, and overcome the villain to save their world. Before the hero can triumph, he or she must gain some new kind of knowledge, which brings with it great power. The hero invariably has a group of loyal friends who make up a hero team, ever devoted to his or her success in the battles against evil. Who wouldn't like to live a life like that? I know I would! Isn't that one reason we love hero tales, because they cause us to consider and aspire toward a life of great excitement and reward, a life in which we overcome evil with good?

CHARACTERISTICS OF THE CLASSIC HERO

- The classic hero starts out as an ordinary, imperfect individual beset by character flaws and weaknesses common to all of us.

- Once in the extraordinary world or situation, the hero exhibits extraordinary abilities, talents or powers.

- In the course of the journey, the hero learns much and is transformed through tests, trials and experiences.

- The hero values love and compassion, and must grow to exhibit these honored qualities.

- The hero aligns with good in the battle against evil—as it is defined within the story.

- The hero usually exemplifies society's highest values: typically these include bravery, loyalty, friendship, persistence and kindness, but can also include things such as fame, wealth and hard work.

- The hero eventually sacrifices himself or herself to save others. Usually this involves saving more than just one person but an entire society or world.

- The hero inspires heroism in others, in the hero team and in the reader.

HOPE FOR ALL OF US WOULD-BE HEROES

One of the most wonderful things about the leading characters of fantastic stories is that they are basically ordinary at the start of the story. Classic heroes are endearing in part because they are not perfect; they start out just as flawed as the rest of us. This gives hope to the would-be heroes among us.

Before Peter, Susan, Edmund and Lucy became kings and queens in Narnia, they had spats like most brothers and sisters. The older ones chided the younger ones; the younger ones resented it. Edmund, as the younger brother, delighted in aggravating his siblings and was downright spiteful to Lucy.

Even though *Star Wars* is set in a galaxy far, far away, who among us can't relate to the impulsiveness of youth we see in Luke Skywalker? He's so eager to head off into the world to make his mark, he doesn't fully appreciate all Aunt Beru and Uncle Owen have done for him. He seems a bit selfish, like the rest of us. We connect with that desire to do something that makes us more important than others. We too chafe at having to simply do our duty.

It's obvious Harry is not perfect. He spent his childhood being convinced that he is the opposite of special. As we get to know Harry Potter we see that he has to put up with a lot, but he also lets his anger get away with him. He talks back, he lies at times to cover his tracks, and he goads his cousin (although that is well deserved). Even if we can't relate to his plight of being an orphan or being merely tolerated by his wretched aunt, uncle, and cousin, we probably relate to losing our temper when we are severely provoked, or covering our tracks to stay out of trouble (although we don't usually call this lying when we think of our own social maneuvering).

We can relate to these characters *because* they are not perfect, living in imperfect circumstances, and longing for more out of life. Don't we all?

HEROES IN *STAR WARS*

Let's look at how Luke Skywalker, the primary hero of *Star Wars,* measures up to the classic characteristics of a hero. Luke showed human weakness in being over-eager to get into the Academy, wanting to shirk his duty of helping with the harvest. He seemed to lack proper appreciation toward his aunt and uncle, given that they had taken him in, cared for his needs and raised him well. Not unlike others of his age—whether on Tatooine or planet Earth—he seems self-absorbed and a bit reckless.

Luke began with no apparent extraordinary ability. He was a good flyer, but it was only as he developed his gifts and practiced using the Force that his abilities became exceptional. Yet he was always extraordinary, by virtue of his birth. Luke didn't know it, but he was born a child of the chosen one. That's why Obi-Wan, Yoda and Senator Organa went to such pains to hide him. He was born with a great destiny, but that transformation was brought about through his experiences along the path of his hero's journey.

In Luke we see the highly valued qualities of bravery, loyalty to his friends—like when he left the Dagoba System to rescue Han Solo and Leia even though this displeased Yoda—and skill as a warrior. He grows from being selfish to becoming selfless, showing great courage and daring in the face of enormous personal risk as he flew into the belly of the Death Star to destroy it and protect the worlds it threatened throughout the galaxy.

Self-sacrifice is probably the crowning virtue associated with the hero. Luke risked his life trying to rescue Princess Leia from Darth Vader. When he had to choose between death and turning to the dark side, he chose to fall—to his apparent death—rather than to give in to evil. He learned this virtue from his mentors and hero team. There are numerous examples of self-sacrifice among the heroes of *Star Wars.* Obi-Wan Kenobi allowed himself to be killed in battle against Darth Vader so that

Luke, Leia and Han Solo could escape. Princess Leia risked her life attacking Jabba the Hutt (and managing to kill him) after her failed attempt to rescue Han Solo.

Luke's relentless love, determination to fight against the dark side and courage to stand firm in this resolve inspired heroism in others. Together Luke and Leia were able to inspire Han Solo to return to the Rebel Alliance and aid the rebellion against the Empire. Under the leadership of Luke's hero team (which includes Chewbacca, R2-D2 and C-3PO), Lando Calrissian and the Ewoks were encouraged to rise up against the Empire.

By the end of the stories, Luke is transformed into a full-fledged Jedi, changed by what he has learned from his mentors Obi-Wan Kenobi and Yoda, but also from his experiences in battles against the various manifestations of evil power, and through his expanding understanding of his own history. His transformation includes a growing knowledge of the Force and the Jedi Code, but also a better, more mature understanding of himself. He learns to rein in his anger and develop self-control, and grows to have loving compassion even for his father and avowed enemy, Darth Vader. That love empowers Luke to resist the dark side of the Force and inspire what is left of his father to finally break free from the dark side, destroying the evil Emperor while sacrificing his own life in the process. His father ultimately appears in the spirit realm beside Yoda and Obi-Wan Kenobi as Anakin, the young Jedi he had been before turning to the dark side.

To think of all the good Luke Skywalker was able to accomplish, even though it is a fantasy, is encouraging to the rest of us would-be heroes who relate to him before he became a hero.

HEROES IN THE CHRONICLES OF NARNIA

C. S. Lewis wrote the Chronicles of Narnia primarily for children, so it is not surprising that children are cast as the heroes in all seven of the stories: Digory and Polly, the Pevensie children, Eustace and Jill. Since *The Lion, The Witch and The Wardrobe* is most familiar, I'll start there.

When we first meet Peter, Susan, Edmund and Lucy, they are well- behaved and properly brought-up British children, but they are not without apparent character flaws and human foibles. These brothers and sisters have their share of squabbles and rivalry. In Edmund we see a vulnerability to deception and evil influences. Through the effect of Narnian air, the power of the prophecies, and their battles, training and contact with Aslan, their transformation into heroes begins, and they become kings and queens of Narnia, with extraordinary gifts and abilities, wisdom, wealth and power. Their previous petty squabbles give way to regal bearing, loyalty to and love for each other, their subjects and Aslan.

The self-sacrifice of the hero is covered in *The Lion, the Witch and the Wardrobe* first by Aslan. Edmund is in clear violation of ancient laws, and the witch claims the right to his blood. None of the children is qualified to ransom him from death. Aslan, who knows the deeper magic, sacrifices himself. But he rises again to join them in battle. There at the Battle of Beruna all four children prove themselves heroes, demonstrating remarkable bravery and skill as they risk their lives in service to Aslan and to protect Narnia from evil. No one proves more heroic than Edmund, who destroys the White Witch's wand. He is severely wounded, and only Lucy's vial of magical ointment heals him. All four of these Narnian heroes inspire the creatures on Aslan's side, and the battle is won.

These children, and the children who star as heroes of the other chronicles, start out fully human, weak and flawed, but grow through their respective journeys. They inspire readers, especially other children: they are human enough for us to relate to them and heroic enough to inspire us to fight and win our personal battles against evil.

HEROES IN HARRY POTTER STORIES

Harry Potter is the primary hero in the stories that bear his name, although there are many characters on his hero team who behave hero-ically. It is clear that we follow Harry's journey because each book goes through one year after another of his education at Hogwarts, where he is receiving his training as a wizard. Harry starts out a sympathetic character, given all he has endured with his parents' murders and abusive relatives. However, he is clearly imperfect.

Every classic hero has a weakness; Harry has many. I see Harry as "every man" or in his case, "every kid." As Harry's detractors (in his world and ours) have pointed out, Harry has been known to lie, break rules, sneak out and occasionally be thoughtless toward others while thinking of what he wants. In *Harry Potter and the Prisoner of Azkaban*, he puts everyone at Hogwarts at risk by sneaking out to Hogsmead without permission while suspected murderer Sirius Black is at large.

Harry definitely has some weak spots when it comes to his conduct. However, so do most teens as they work through making their own decisions. This is why I see Harry as being so well-loved by young people. He starts out like them, but he chooses to join the good side, takes his stand against evil and learns to do better.

Harry Potter is such a classic hero that his enemy can predict what he will do, which leaves him vulnerable. In *Harry Potter and the Order of the Phoenix*, Harry's friend Hermione Granger tries to get him to recognize that his dream of an ally being tortured at the Ministry of Magic might be a trap set by the villain Voldemort.

"You . . . This isn't a criticism, Harry! But you do . . . sort of . . . I mean—don't you think you've got a bit of a—*saving-people-thing?*" she said.

He glared at her. "And what's that supposed to mean, a 'saving-people-thing?'"

"Well . . . you . . . ." She looked more apprehensive than ever. "I mean . . . last year, for instance . . . in the lake . . . during the Tournament . . . you shouldn't have . . . I mean, you didn't need to save that little Delacour girl . . . You got a bit . . . carried away . . ."

A wave of hot, prickly anger swept Harry's body—how could she remind him of that blunder now?

". . . I mean, it was really great of you and everything," said Hermione quickly, looking positively petrified at the look on Harry's face. "Everyone thought it was a wonderful thing to do–"

"That's funny," said Harry through gritted teeth, "because I definitely remember Ron saying I'd wasted time *acting the hero* . . . is that what you think this is? You reckon I want to act the hero again?"

"No, no, no!" said Hermione, looking aghast. "That's not what I mean at all!"

"Well spit out what you've got to say, because we're wasting time here!" Harry shouted.

"I'm trying to say—Voldemort knows you, Harry! He took Ginny down into the Chamber of Secrets to lure you there, it's the kind of thing he does, he knows you're the—the sort of person who'd go to Sirius's aid!

Here we see how even Harry's classic heroic tendencies have become a point of vulnerability for him. Once in the extraordinary world, the hero exhibits extraordinary abilities, talents or powers. Harry does not recognize his extraordinary abilities at the beginning. He discovers his magical powers when Hagrid tells him that he is a wizard, but even before he knew why, he could make strange things happen. In *Harry Potter and the Sorcerer's Stone,* for example, Harry's high emotion causes Dudley to fall into the snake enclosure without him intending for that to happen. Once Harry begins training at Hogwarts he is able to develop his natural magical abilities, learning to use his wand, fly on a broomstick and become invisible, among other things.

While Harry does not have the exceptional physical powers or strength often associated with heroes, his natural attributes become assets to his adventures. In the muggle (or natural) world, being small was a detriment to Harry. His grossly large cousin, Dudley, repeatedly beat him up, and he was chosen last for sports. In the wizarding world, however, being small and agile becomes a plus, helping Harry battle a large mountain troll or zip around dodging bludgers and catching the snitch in Quidditch. He was chosen to be the seeker for the school Quidditch team in his first year because of his natural agility on a broomstick, making him the youngest school seeker in a hundred years.

Harry starts out with plenty of compassion, sharing candy from the cart with new friend Ron Weasley, who doesn't have spending money. He understands how it feels to be deprived of luxuries because his aunt and uncle never gave him money for candy or anything else. So he shares his inherited fortune generously. He starts aligning himself with good and eschewing evil even before he gets to Hogwarts, by his aversion to the bully Draco Malfoy. Having been bullied himself, Harry risks getting in trouble to protect Neville Longbottom—a weaker kid—from Draco, who tries to throw away the boy's prized possession, the Remembrall. When placed under the Sorting Hat to determine which house he would live in, Harry's insistence, "Not Slytherin! Not Slytherin!" helps to place him in Gryffindor. Harry is devoted to Gryffindor, Hogwarts and his beloved headmaster Dumbledore. Harry grows in love throughout the series this turns out to be his most powerful weapon against Voldemort, according to Dumbledore. It was his mother's love that had protected him in the beginning, but as he grows he develops his own store of this most powerful quality.

Harry is staunchly opposed to the one who would destroy their world, and he is working on developing good character. He is determined to stay on the good side and be good; but it takes practice. Harry learns much as he goes along about the use of magic and defense against the dark arts, but also about his history, his destiny and making good choices. It is this process of learning to make good choices—sometimes from the consequences of making poor ones—that facilitates his transformation. He grows from wanting vengeance against his parents' murderer to choosing to prevent his parents' betrayer from being killed: his parents, he reasons, would not approve of murder. We see Harry grow to understand his responsibility to fight and defeat Voldemort.

Harry exemplifies society's highest values: bravery, loyalty, friendship, hard work, persistence, and kindness. Although he goes through typical teenaged angst and moodiness, we see him gradually gain self-control and show bravery in many ways, particularly in that he is the only one—besides Dumbledore—who is not afraid to say Voldemort's name. Harry practices hard to develop his natural skills in Quidditch. He works hard in school and proves to be an extremely loyal friend. Even though Harry is famous and wealthy, he remains kind to those whom others looked down on, like Neville and Luna Lovegood. Harry Potter is keen to sacrifice himself to protect the wizarding world or rescue someone he cares about: Hermione from a mountain troll, Ginny from a Basilisk, Mr. Weasley from a snake, and Ron, Hermione and Gabrielle from drowning.

We follow Harry as he develops into the hero, but we also meet many heroes whom he admires and emulates. Some of Harry's heroism is surely inspired by his parents, both of whom gave their lives in the fight against Voldemort and the Death Eaters. Dumbledore repeatedly sacrifices himself in Harry's fifth and sixth year. And while Harry never tells anyone to be brave or heroic, he inspires heroism and self-sacrifice in others. In *Sorcerer's Stone,* for example, Ron sacrifices himself, in a life-sized game of chess against powerful and vicious pieces, so that Harry and Hermione can get through. In *Chamber of Secrets* Harry secures the release of Dobby the indentured house-elf, who then enjoys a life of freedom and dignity. Harry is an inspiration to many of the students at Hogwarts, particularly best friends Ron and Hermione. At one point, Harry commends Neville, inspiring him to stand up for himself against bullies Crabbe and Goyle. As the story proceeds, so does Neville. He begins as a sorry excuse for a wizard, or so it seems, with his forgetfulness and apparent lack of abilities. However, his contribution puts Gryffindor over the top in the competition between houses during Harry's first year. Neville becomes more daring, accomplished, brave and—following Harry's lead—more heroic in the escalating battles against evil.

The classic hero is a rescuer, or savior of a society, not simply of one individual. The wizarding world is threatened by Voldemort and the Death Eaters, and repeatedly Harry must face Voldemort to keep him from gaining absolute power and to protect the good in wizarding society. We aren't privy to the end of Harry's story as I write this, but I am confident that in the series' final volume J. K. Rowling will not disappoint us, and Harry's transformation from an ordinary boy into a full-fledged hero will be complete.

We see in the heroes of *Star Wars,* Narnia and Harry Potter characteristics common to classic mythic heroes as each battles evil in their own fantastic world. Being familiar with their less than heroic beginnings, we are not surprised to see that these characters start out like ourselves—as human beings with all the weaknesses inherent in that state—but became heroes through their ongoing battle to resist and overcome evil. We expect this of our fantasy heroes; however, many are surprised to see that people in the Bible also share our human condition, undergo a hero's journey and become heroes in their battles against evil.

HEROES IN THE BIBLE'S HALL OF FAME

There is a chapter in the Bible (Hebrews 11) that is referred to as "Heroes of Faith" or the "Faith Hall of Fame." Listed in Hebrews 11 are some of the greatest men and women in the Bible: Abraham, Sarah, Isaac, Jacob, Noah, Samson, Gideon, and others whose names have been renowned for generations. Most of us think of Bible heroes as holy and righteous, sporting shining halos in old paintings. However, a careful check shows that they share the common condition of classic heroes at the beginning of their stories: imperfection. The Bible reveals that they all had character flaws and moral weaknesses at some point in their journey. But all crossed the threshold into the extraordinary to exhibit extraordinary faith and supernatural powers, and all did their part in the battle to overcome evil with good. In the course of their journeys each one learned and was transformed into a true hero whom God was not ashamed to single out as an example for us.

Lest you think I exaggerate, let's take a look at some of their character flaws and failings in order to better appreciate how far they came to become heroes and affirm that there is hope for all of us:

- Noah got drunk and exposed himself to whoever happened into his tent (Genesis 9:21-23).

- Abraham and his son Isaac both lied, saying their wives were their sisters, protecting themselves while putting their wives at greater risk (Genesis 12:11-12; 20:2; 26:7-9).

- Sarah, the wife of Abraham, was so jealous and embittered against her servant girl Hagar that she insisted Abraham send the young woman and her son out into the desert to die (think of Sarah from Hagar's son's perspective; can you spell W-I-C-K-E-D S-T-E-P-M-O-T-H-E-R? Genesis 21:9, 14-16).

- Jacob used a disguise and blatant lies to trick his blind father and effectively steal his elder brother's birthright (Genesis 27:19).

- Joseph was so puffed up by his father's favoritism that he became arrogant—so much so that his brothers wanted to kill him and were only barely persuaded rather to sell him as a slave (Genesis 37:5-11, 26-27).

- Moses committed murder (Exodus 2:14-16).

- Rahab was a prostitute (some people even fault her for lying when men of Jericho came looking for the Hebrew spies she had hidden;

Joshua 2:4-6).

- Barak, a general in the army of Israel, was afraid to go into battle unless Deborah the judge went with him (some might call that cowardly; Judges 4:8-9).

- Samson spent most of his life chasing foreign women and disregarding his parent's wishes (Judges 14:3). He was out of control sexually, giving in to the lures of Delilah (Judges 16:3-16) and violently misusing his supernatural strength (Judges 15:4, 15-16).

- Gideon started out hiding in a hole in the ground and questioning the value of God's miracles since he had never seen any (Judges 6:11).

- David committed adultery (2 Samuel 11:1-3), and then effectively murdered one of his most loyal soldiers, by arranging to have him killed in battle, to cover up his sin (2 Samuel 11:14-17).

Each person on this list and others in Hebrews 11 went on to demonstrate extraordinary powers and gain special knowledge, and were transformed by the things they experienced in the course of their journey. They grew in love, found their place on the side of good, and came to exemplify the life of faith and other highly esteemed qualities. Each took his or her place on God's side in the ongoing struggle against evil. Thus their lives can be used by God to inspire the rest of us. Hebrews 11:32-39 catalogues highlights of their heroic feats:

- some conquered kingdoms
- some performed acts of righteousness
- some obtained promises from God
- some shut the mouths of lions
- some quenched the power of fire
- some escaped the edge of the sword
- some were made strong from weakness
- some became mighty in war

- some put foreign armies to flight
- some received back their dead by resurrection
- some were tortured, not accepting their release in order that they might obtain a better resurrection
- some experienced mocking, scourging, chains and imprisonment
- some were stoned to death
- some (the prophet Isaiah, for example) were sawn in two
- some were tempted
- some were put to death with the sword
- some were destitute, afflicted and ill-treated, dressing in the skins of sheep and goats
- some wandered in deserts, mountains, caves, and holes in the ground

After this list of heroic living and miraculous feats the Bible declares that the world was not worthy of them. "These were all commended for their faith, yet none of them received what had been promised. God had planned something better for us so that only together with us would they be made perfect" (Hebrews 11:39-40).

What does this mean to us? These Old Testament heroes of faith were part of a larger story, a story that spanned their generations and Christ's generation, and benefits our generation. Each had their own battles to fight and part to play within those battles, some even as ancestors in the lineage of the Messiah. Thus they were used by God to help to bring Christ to Earth to give his sinless life as a sacrifice, overthrow the curse of death, and offer salvation and eternal life to all who would believe.

So each Old Testament hero of faith and the battles they fought are connected to us. We're all part of a larger story composed by the Great Storyteller. The way these heroes trusted God and fought their battles encourages and instructs us. Similarly, the way we fight our battles will have bearing on the lives and faith of those who come after us and hear our stories, until Christ returns in final triumph.

These Bible heroes, some of whom started their story in obscurity or infamy, went on to inspire others throughout history and around the world. We can trace their transformation over the course of their journeys. The fact that such as these could be empowered to play important parts in God's story, written in human lives, inspires me. Their journey brought each of them to the status of heroes of faith, but also brought to us the opportunity to cross the threshold—through the door of faith—into an extraordinary world. We too can experience the power of the Holy Spirit that empowered and transformed their lives, and likewise become mighty agents of God, playing a part in the ongoing cosmic battle between good and evil.

IS THERE HOPE FOR US AS WOULD-BE HEROES? BELIEVE IT!

Might there really be hope for any of us—even those with humble beginnings—to see our lives transformed into heroic tales of triumph? Be careful how you answer this, even to yourself. Our expectations of what our lives may or should become will have tremendous impact on how we face our battles. It can determine whether we fulfill the purpose and potential for our lives. In short, if you don't believe your life is meant to be a hero's journey it probably won't; if you do it might amaze you and inspire others in the end.

This story serves as an illustration. A young man in his mid-twenties was severely depressed, so much so that his closest companions worried he might attempt suicide. One of his dearest friends broached the subject with him. He told his friend that he had "done nothing to make any human being remember that he had lived," and that he desired to "connect his name with the events transpiring in his day and generation, and so impress himself upon them as to link his name with something that would redound to the interest of his fellow man." He could not end his life before he had done something for the good of his fellows, something that would cause his life to be remembered and be an inspiration to others. He went on to become one of my heroes, and a hero to many Americans and lovers of freedom everywhere. His name was Abraham Lincoln.

Apparently, even when deeply depressed, Lincoln held firmly to the belief that his life was meant to make a difference. I am so glad he held out for the heroic and did not give in to his suicidal feelings, but pressed on past all the terrible tests and trials he faced to accomplish that which did "link his name with something that would redound to the interest of his fellow man." Decades after the above conversation took place Lincoln reminisced with his friend, Joshua F. Speed, with whom he had that conversation. Now as President, Lincoln discussed the Emancipation Proclamation with Speed, saying with earnest emphasis, "I believe that in this measure my fondest hope will be realized."[1] What might you or I do if we firmly believe that we must not die until we have done our part to overcome the evils of our times?

Most of us who read heroic stories have fueled our imaginations with lofty aspirations, dreams of grandeur and hopes for the heroic. We may not have known the depths of despair that might drive someone to consider suicide. However, even in our darkest hours, we need to believe that each of our lives was made for more than serving ourselves. We are here for a good purpose! We all were created as would-be heroes. God longs to write the story of our lives so that good triumphs over evil. Therefore, the more we align ourselves with God's good story for our lives, the better off we will be. When times get rough, we need to see the story through until God's fondest hopes for us are realized and evil is overcome with good.

In each life resides the possibility of overcoming evil with good. That will only be realized by those who answer the call. Now let's look at where the heroes of Harry Potter, The Chronicles of Narnia and *Star*

Wars began their journeys. Let's look at their life in the ordinary world. Have you ever thought, *There has to be more to life than this!*? Who among us—while mired in the ordinariness of everyday life—doesn't hope for more? Life is supposed to be exciting, right? That's what we've always seen in the movies and read about in story books. And yet if we take a closer look at the kind of stories we love, with exciting heroes and daring journeys, they usually start from a mundane beginning, although set against a backdrop of abuse or danger. Their mundane starting point allows us, in our ordinary lives, to connect with the hero-to-be; the ordinary beginnings provide contrast to the adventures about to begin. We dream of other worlds, pretend to adventures or simply wonder at life beyond (whether in a galaxy far, far away, at Hogwarts or through the wardrobe).

ORDINARY CHARACTERS IN THEIR ORDINARY WORLD

At the beginning of their story most heroes-to-be are living everyday lives: boring, difficult, frustrating and ordinary, with no indication life will ever be different. The main character is usually in danger, whether or not they yet recognize it, or sustaining ongoing abuse.

In *The Magician's Nephew* Digory Kirke has been sent, along with his ailing mother, to live with his aunt and a mad uncle. He meets Polly Plummer while trying to hide that he has been crying because his mother is dying. According to the story, "Their adventures began chiefly because it was one of the wettest and coldest summers there had been for years. That drove them to do indoor . . . exploration." At the beginning of *Prince Caspian* the four Pevensie children are sitting on a seat at a sleepy railway station, waiting for the trains that would take them to their respective schools. At the very moment they were about to be called back into Narnia, they were feeling gloomy, totally unexpectant. At the start of *The Voyage of the "Dawn Treader,"* Lucy and Edmund Pevensie are sent to stay with Aunt Alberta, Uncle Harold and their obnoxious cousin Eustace Clarence Scrubb. The picture in the room where Lucy was staying reminds them of a Narnian ship, but they wonder if it isn't worse to be looking at a Narnian ship when they can't get there. Eustace comes in and begins to tease them about their "imaginary" land. None of them expects that in a moment the ship will come to life, and they will all three be drawn into the icy sea and a great adventure. At the start of *The Silver Chair,* Jill Pole is behind the gym at Experiment House, crying because students were bullying her. Eustace Scrubb, now a different boy after his first visit to Narnia but used to being abused by the bullies at their school, shares his secret with her. They hear the bullies approaching and run toward the hedges, not expecting to cross over into Narnia.

It was an ordinary day. And so it goes. Heroic stories usually start with an ordinary—although often troubled—time of life.

In a way, this is one of my favorite parts of a fantasy story. Whenever bored on a rainy day, those who've read *The Lion, the Witch and the Wardrobe* can recall that on just such an ordinary afternoon the Pevensie children opened the door to another world. Those familiar with *Star Wars,* feeling frustrated by their restrictive circumstances, feeling a pent-up desire to break free and do something significant, can recall that Luke Skywalker started out there, before he was propelled into his adventure. Those who have commiserated with Harry Potter, pulling spiders from his hair in his cupboard under the stairs, can relate their feelings of being abused, neglected or underappreciated to his, and remember that life didn't leave him there. We—like the characters we've connected with—all start out in the ordinary world, facing various levels of danger. Fantastic stories give us hope that our ordinary lives can become extraordinary.

Bible Characters Before the Extraordinary Breaks Through

The Bible gives us many examples of ordinary people, living mundane, boring, difficult or endangered lives—until something breaks in that changes everything and ends up transforming them into heroes. If we have heard their stories at all, we probably remember their heroic deeds rather than the ordinariness of their lives *before* their adventures began.

An old man, definitely past his prime. How long had it been since he came across that desert? How many years, thirty-nine or forty? How long since he met the daughters of the priest who didn't know his name or his former glory. They thought of him simply as a wandering Egyptian until he chased off some shepherds so they could water their flock. How long since people bowed before him? Now, at his feet, there were only bleating sheep, goats and burning sand. He had his family—his wife, her sisters and father. He had a son, whose name reflected what he had become: *Gershom,* an outcast. He was an old man with only memories of former glory.

Day after blistering day, he wandered the desert tending his father-in-law's flocks. What did he expect? He'd tried to play the hero but had to flee for his life when he killed an Egyptian. He was lucky to be alive, lucky Pharaoh's guards hadn't caught and killed him. Perhaps. He certainly had plenty of time to think about what might have been. At least that distracted him from the monotony of leading flocks another day in this scorching wasteland. Yes, Moses had it pretty bad in his ordinary life *before* his call.

Disillusioned youth. The young man was living with his father, reduced to hiding in a hole in the ground. For the past seven years he and his people had been humiliated by their enemies. Dependent on an agricultural economy, they planted crops of wheat, cultivated their fields and hoped for a harvest they could keep. When the harvest would come and it was time to thresh their wheat they dared not do it out in the open, tossing it into the air where the wind would carry away the chaff. Their enemies were waiting for them to get all the work done processing the wheat before they would swoop down on them to steal all they'd worked for, all they depended on to survive. Year after year their more powerful neighbors had come at harvest time, stolen the fruit of their labors, killed their livestock and destroyed their goods, along with their morale.

In order to protect the harvest, this youngest son took the wheat down into a wine vat, a pit in the ground. Without the help of the wind he had to work much harder to thresh it. He certainly was not singing songs of thanksgiving or praising God. He was resentful, afraid, frustrated. But what could he do? He didn't think he could change the status quo. His family was one of the least powerful in their tribe, which was one of the least in their clan, which was least in Israel.

When that young man got up that morning, took his pitchfork in calloused hands, and headed down into the wine press to hide while he tried to do his part for his family, he did not expect anything extraordinary to happen. Disillusioned? You bet. Grumbling? Yep. He had heard the miracle stories at his mother's knee, heard old men telling the tales around the fire late into the night. God led his forefathers out of slavery in Egypt. Even if God had sent the plagues, parted the Red Sea and led the Hebrews through the wilderness, providing water in the desert and sending food from open skies, what was that to him on that morning? He was literally stuck in a rut, working hard to sift out a little wheat he assumed their enemies would steal. Where was God when the enemies attacked, where were the miracles when he needed one? He wasn't full of faith that God was going to come to the rescue.

It never crossed his mind that he might be the hero God would use to change everything and save his people from their enemies. Young Gideon—frustrated, disillusioned, upset, fearful, basically hopeless—is someone we can relate to. If that kid's ordinary life could suddenly become extraordinary, there's hope for anyone.

The trapped prostitute. Her city was abuzz with rumors of a powerful tribe about to attack. Everyone was terrified. They had heard of their mighty God. When two spies arrived at her door and the harlot hid them, then lied to her own people to protect the spies, she did not know what would become of her. At that point in her story who would have imagined that Rahab would save the lives of her loved ones, turn to God and go on to become the great-great-grandmother of a great king and one whose name would be recorded in the lineage of the Messiah (in Matthew 1:5)?

The baby of the family. Being the youngest, he was left to do the boring job of staying in the fields with his father's sheep when the prophet Samuel came to their house. It was only after all seven of his brothers had been rejected by the prophet that they even considered bringing in the baby of the family.

When the call to battle came and all the young men were drafted into service, his seven brothers headed for the battlefield; he was left at home with his aging father. He might have thought, *Why do I have to stay home? It's not fair!* Despite his protests, the youngest of eight had to do his daily chores, wondering what exciting adventures he was missing. The only thing he was fighting was resentment. He knew he was as strong as them and far braver. He wanted to show them, someday . . . if he ever got the chance.

No one took young David seriously, until the Prophet Samuel anointed him as the future king and King Saul called on him to slay a giant.

On the verge of the extraordinary. None of these characters realized that their ordinary lives were on the verge of the extraordinary. Each one had no idea he or she was about to experience something that would cast them into the annals of fantastic stories, heroes, and miracles. It was just another day. Some were living disappointed, angry, disillusioned or frustrated lives. Some were grateful to be alive, others didn't much care anymore. All were probably wondering at times, *Is this all there is to life? Is this the way the story will go until it ends?*

Once we know their stories, we know nothing could be further from the truth. Moses, the old man tending flocks in the desert, was about to see a fire that would set the world ablaze with hope of freedom. Gideon, the disillusioned youth, was about to have an encounter that would propel him to become the mighty warrior he'd never have believed he could be. Rahab, the prostitute of Jericho, would become a vital part in the bloodline of the promised Messiah. David, the baby of the family, would go on to slay a giant, become one of the greatest kings the world has ever known, and start a dynasty that will last forever.

WHEN LIFE IN THE ORDINARY WORLD IS TOUGH . . .

Knowing fantastic stories gives us hope when our lives are boring, unpromising or difficult. Whether fantasy stories or true Bible stories, their mundane beginnings give us hope when we need assurance that there is more to life than what is apparent in our ordinary lives.

We were made for a purpose. There is a battle going on between good and evil in our world and in the spiritual realm, and God calls us to join the action on the side of good against the forces of evil. Next, let's look at that call.

2

The Call to Join the Battle Against Evil

"Your task will be the harder because of what you
have done."

"Please, what task sir?" said Jill.

"The task for which I called you and him here out
of your own world."

Aslan to Jill, The Silver Chair

"Come, follow me."

Jesus (Mark 1:17)

Have you ever seen a child play at being a princess or a prince who must
win back his lost kingdom? Much of the drama and pretending in childhood is spent imagining (or, these days, playing a video game) about
some grand adventure or battle. I think we all long for a calling, for
someone "out there" to set us apart for some special purpose. I also believe that we struggle with the desire to stay safe, even going so far as to
create a home out of the way of danger, like when the Pevensie children
were sent away from London during the air raids in *The Lion, the Witch
and the Wardrobe.* Even hidden away, there in the country they could not
escape the battle between good and evil. This tug-of-war between want-

ing to make our mark in life, to do something significant, versus wanting to stay safely out of the fray is perhaps why we relate so well to our soon-to-be heroes.

THE HERALD

Most heroes are called into their adventures by a herald. This mythic archetype brings a message, announces a challenge, delivers an invitation or otherwise calls heroes into action. According to Christopher Vogler in *A Writer's Journey,* a herald doesn't have to be a person.[1] It can be a force of nature, animals like owls in *Harry Potter,* even a technological device such as the holographic recording of Princess Leia's plea for help in *Star Wars: A New Hope.* Anything that serves the function of calling our hero and motivating him or her to get the story moving, acts as the herald.

We usually see the herald at the beginning of the story. Once the herald has delivered the call, nothing can go back to the way it was before. Luke Skywalker and Obi-Wan Kenobi see and hear the holographic pleas of Princess Leia, desperately calling for their help to get the droid to Alderon: What will they do? In *Harry Potter and the Sorcerer's Stone,* Hagrid says, "You're a wizard, Harry," and delivers the overdue invitation to Hogwarts; Harry must decide to stay with the Dursleys or answer the call into the wizarding world. Lucy tells Peter, Susan and Edmund about Narnia; they have to decide to believe her or not. Once all four get to Narnia, they are heralded further by the arrest decree found in faun Tumnus's ransacked cave. They find themselves in the middle of a struggle between good and evil; they must either try to help the faun or turn their backs on his plight. But once the call arrives there is no going back to life as it was before the call.

The hero must respond, act or react, believe or disbelieve. The herald is usually sent by someone; Hagrid is sent by Dumbledore, and R2-D2 is sent by Princess Leia. However, there can be unwitting heralds who unintentionally deliver a call to adventure. In *The Magician's Nephew,*

Digory and Polly venture into the world of Charn by jumping into a pool in the Wood between the Worlds. Charn seems to be a dead world; they find figures of former royalty seated in a royal hall. Digory is drawn by an enchanted verse to take up a small hammer and strike a bell:

Make your choice, adventurous Stranger.
Strike the bell and bide the danger,
Or wonder, till it drives you mad,
What would have followed if you had.

In one sense, the verse itself is a herald, presenting a challenge Digory could not resist. He strikes the bell and awakens Jadis, Queen of Charn. Although unaware of what he was about to do, Digory became the herald who called Jadis back to life. For the rest of *The Magician's Nephew* and *The Lion, the Witch and the Wardrobe*—in which Jadis is known as the White Witch—there is no going back. Jadis barrels into the story, into London and eventually into Narnia, and gets the story moving, thus requiring heroes to rise up on the side of good to oppose her.

REFUSAL OF THE CALL

Most who are called by a herald have a time of hesitation. The would-be hero struggles with doubts or refuses the call.

In *The Lion, the Witch and the Wardrobe* Lucy calls her sister and brothers to follow her into Narnia. They try the wardrobe, but initially it is closed to them. Since they can't see what she saw, they don't believe her. They dismiss her story as silly fantasizing, even worrying that she has lost her mind. Later, when all four are in Narnia, they see that Mr. Tumnus, the faun who befriended Lucy, has been arrested. Circumstances and honor call them to try to right what happened to Mr. Tumnus, yet all but Lucy hesitate, considering the dangers and looking back toward the wardrobe. Will they answer the call with its attendant dangers or go back while they still can?

In *Star Wars: A New Hope,* young Luke Skywalker ventures away from the safety of his home with Aunt Beru and Uncle Owen in search of the wayward droid, R2-D2, who has set out to complete his "secret mission." C-3PO and Luke dismiss such talk as errant babbling; Luke only pursues R2-D2 so he doesn't get in trouble with his uncle for letting the droid wander off. Luke is attacked but rescued by "Old Ben Kenobi," a strange and mysterious hermit. He tells Ben that the droid seems to be searching for Obi-Wan Kenobi to deliver a holographic message from a beautiful young woman.

"Obi-Wan," Kenobi says, "Now that's a name I have not heard in a long time. . . . Of course, I know him. He is me. I haven't gone by that name . . . oh, since before you were born." He goes on to reveal that he had been a Jedi Knight alongside Luke's father, with whom he fought in the Clone Wars. He gives Luke his father's light saber, saying his father wanted him to have it, and speaks of the glory days: "For over a thousand generations the Jedi Knights were the guardians of peace and justice in the Old Republic, before the dark times, before the Empire." Together, Obi-Wan and Luke watch the full message sent by Princess Leia, who pleads with Obi-Wan Kenobi to deliver the droid—and its secreted plans—safely to her father on Alderon.

Obi-Wan Kenobi then tells Luke, "You must learn the ways of the Force if you are to come with me to Alderon."

Luke, taken aback, protests firmly, giving a list of reasons that he couldn't go. Obi-Wan responds, "I need your help, Luke. She needs your help."

Luke insists, "I can't get involved. I've got work to do."

Obi-Wan relents. "You must do what you feel is right, of course." Still he urges Luke to learn about the Force.

Luke is torn: he longs to follow his father's course and join the resistance, but he also feels a duty to his uncle, who relies on his help with the harvest. Only when he returns home to find the place smoldering, devastated, his aunt and uncle murdered by Imperial Storm Troopers, does he choose to follow the call and go with Obi-Wan to Alderon.

Most people can relate to this phase of a fantastic story. Self-doubt and hesitation are common to us all. We may long for adventure, to join the battle against evil in our realm, but we hardly believe we can really make a difference. We may fear danger or worry that we don't have what it takes to complete the journey laid before us. Maybe we can't yet relate to the amazing tales of adventure, transformation and supernatural battles, but surely all of us can relate to heroes who hesitate.

BIBLE HEROES WHO HESITATED AT THE CALL

Perhaps it will make us feel better to know that it's not just our fantasy heroes who hesitate when called. Even in Bible stories, characters that seem larger than life also sometimes hesitated, finding it hard to believe in things they could not see or simply not understanding the call. If they could get from that point to being transformed into heroes in God's battles, there is hope for us too.

Would-be hero in a hole in the ground. Remember Gideon, the young man from the last chapter who was threshing wheat in a wine vat so his enemies wouldn't steal it? He was in for a surprise that would cause all kinds of hesitation! Here's how the story goes:

> The angel of the LORD came and sat down under the oak in Ophrah that belonged to Joash the Abiezrite, where his son Gideon was threshing wheat in a winepress to keep it from the Midianites. When the angel of the LORD appeared to Gideon, he said, "The LORD is with you, mighty warrior." (Judges 6:11-12)

I find myself wondering if this is a biblical case of sarcasm. The angel was looking down at a scrawny kid, least of the least, hiding in a hole to do his chores. I can think of several appropriate monikers, but "mighty warrior" is definitely not in the top ten. A more spiritual take on this calling might be that the angel was speaking in faith that God was about to make Gideon into a mighty warrior. However, Gideon did not share such an optimistic outlook.

> "But sir," Gideon replied, "if the LORD is with us, why has all this happened to us? Where are all his wonders that our fathers told us about when they said, 'Did not the LORD bring us up out of Egypt?' But now the LORD has abandoned us and put us into the hand of Midian." (Judges 6:13)

It seems Gideon didn't quite catch on to the fact that he was talking to an angel. He saw a man who said to him, "The Lord is with you, mighty warrior." If the Lord was with him, Gideon hadn't noticed. What he had noticed was that he had to do his chores in a hole. His people were under the thumb of ruthless enemies. The stories his fathers had passed down from generation to generation were not making any difference in his situation. So, I guess we can pardon him his note of cynicism.

The next verse says,

> The LORD turned to him and said, "Go in the strength you have and save Israel out of Midian's hand. Am I not sending you?" (Judges 6:14)

Can you imagine what this young man was juggling in his mind? The "man" who appeared atop his hole, called him a mighty warrior and heard his cynical complaints, then suggested that he stop complaining and answer the call to free his nation from their oppressors. Here's his reply:

> "But Lord," Gideon asked, "how can I save Israel? My clan is the weakest in Manasseh, and I am the least in my family."
>
> "The LORD answered, 'I will be with you, and you will strike down all the Midianites together.'" (Judges 6:15-16)

Either someone was playing a serious practical joke or it was definitely a call of the highest order. He wasn't sure, so he asked for a sign.

Gideon replied, "If now I have found favor in your eyes, give me a sign that it is really you talking to me. Please do not go away until I come back and bring my offering and set it before you."

And the LORD said, "I will wait until you return."

(Judges 6:17-18)

Gideon prepared a young goat, made unleavened bread, put the meat in a basket and its broth in a pot, then offered them to the mysterious stranger.

The angel of God said to him, "Take the meat and the unleavened bread, place them on this rock, and pour out the broth." And Gideon did so. With the tip of the staff that was in his hand, the angel of the LORD touched the meat and the unleavened bread. Fire flared from the rock, consuming the meat and the bread. And the angel of the LORD disappeared. When Gideon realized that it was the angel of the LORD, he exclaimed, "Ah, Sovereign LORD! I have seen the angel of the LORD face to face!"

But the LORD said to him, "Peace! Do not be afraid. You are not going to die." (Judges 6:20-23)

Imagine it. Here is a guy we can relate to; he was not expecting anything wonderful to happen, but poof! An angel appeared; he received his call and was supposed to trust God to use *him* to overthrow the enemy oppressing his nation.

What might you do if an angel showed up at your school or workplace and said, "The LORD is with you, mighty warrior"—especially if you were in hiding from the local bully at the time? I think we can relate to his "Yeah, right!" sarcastic reaction. When the Lord said, "Am I not sending you?" I'm sure he had to think about that. He had to be staggered; maybe he thought the Lord had the wrong hole in the ground. Didn't God know *he* couldn't save his nation? Apparently the Lord wasn't looking for human strength. Gideon hesitated, understandably, but the Lord answered by saying, "I will be with you!"

That should settle the matter, for him or for us. But it didn't, and that's one of the reasons I love this guy. He needed another sign, then another, then another before he could bring himself to answer the call. This Gideon is famous for "putting a fleece" before God and saying, *"Well, if you really want me to do this, make the fleece wet and the ground dry."* Then after that request was met—just to be sure—he asked God to make the ground wet and the fleece dry. Finally, reluctantly, he answered his call to adventure.

Maybe we can't relate to the image of the mighty warrior Gideon became; but most of us can relate to the youth who could hardly believe God was calling *him*. We could more easily imagine ourselves saying that perhaps there had been a mistake and that such an important call should be given to someone stronger or more gifted. We can easily relate to wanting to see changes and complaining that God isn't doing enough to help us with our problems. It's a bit more of a stretch to imagine complaining like that and having God reply with a call for us to become the instrument of our own answer to prayer. But that is what happened with Gideon. Likewise, in our lives, we should not be surprised if God calls us to do something to take part in answering the prayers we pray, whether for our provision, our family, our community, our nation, or our world.

Did someone call me? Another Bible character, Samuel, can help us as we consider our call. Long before Israel had a king or a temple, while they were still worshiping God in a tabernacle, Eli was the high priest. His reprobate sons served under him. Even though they officiated as priests, they both misused their power and position horribly. The Lord was about to call the two sons of Eli to account for their wrongdoing.

In the midst of this corruption lived a little boy named Samuel. His mother had promised the Lord that if he would open her womb, she would give him her first-born; Samuel was that miracle child. Once she weaned him, his mother took him to live with Eli and his family at the tabernacle.

Meanwhile, the boy Samuel served the LORD by assisting Eli. Now in those days messages from the LORD were very rare, and visions were quite uncommon.

One night Eli, who was almost blind by now, had gone to bed. The lamp of God had not yet gone out, and Samuel was sleeping in the Tabernacle near the Ark of God. Suddenly, the LORD called out, "Samuel!"

"Yes?" Samuel replied. "What is it?" He jumped up and ran to Eli. "Here I am. Did you call me?"

"I didn't call you," Eli replied. "Go back to bed." So he did. (1 Samuel 3:1-5 NLT)

This happened again as soon as Samuel got back in bed, again he ran to Eli, with the same response. The Bible explains,

"Samuel did not yet know the LORD because he had never had a message from the LORD before. So the LORD called a third time, and once more Samuel got up and went to Eli. "Here I am. Did you call me?"

Then Eli realized it was the LORD who was calling the boy. So he said to Samuel, "Go and lie down again, and if someone calls again, say, 'Speak, LORD, your servant is listening.'" So Samuel went back to bed.

And the LORD came and called as before, "Samuel! Samuel!"

And Samuel replied, "Speak, your servant is listening."

Then the LORD said to Samuel, "I am about to do a shocking thing in Israel. I am going to carry out all my threats against Eli and his family." (1 Samuel 3:7-12 NLT)

Samuel was willing and obedient, but he did not understand the call that he was receiving. It took him hopping out of bed three times before Eli gave him the instruction he needed to heed the call properly.

Aren't the characters in our fantasy stories a bit like this? Digory and Polly in *The Magician's Nephew* were confused at the sight of Uncle Andrew's rings, not comprehending where they might take them. The Pevensie children, even Lucy, were a bit confused by their initial call into Narnia in *The Lion, the Witch and the Wardrobe*. Peter, Susan and Edmund tried to enter Narnia through the wardrobe but found nothing out of the ordinary. In *Harry Potter and the Sorcerer's Stone,* Harry was astounded by Hagrid's call to go to Hogwarts because he didn't understand his heritage, special powers or destiny.

Aren't we a bit like this too, perhaps being called by God to follow him, to enter his kingdom, or for a specific mission or vocation, but not quite sure how to respond. This uncertainty is something all would-be heroes experience. So, as we read fantastic stories and get drawn in by our likeness to those soon-to-be heroes, with their hesitation, fear, frustration, confusion and cynicism, let's consider our lives. Most of us haven't seen angels show up at our workplace, or heard the Lord calling us audibly in our bedroom, so how does this relate to our calling into God's kingdom and the battle against evil?

THE CALL TO FOLLOW CHRIST

More than just a call to follow Christ, which is of primary importance, we want to find God's will for our lives. We—most people, I hope—want to contribute to that which is good and help hold evil at bay. Some people worry that they may miss their calling if they don't hear audible directions from God. We are called to follow Jesus, follow God's word as revealed in the Bible, and take the adventure that comes to us "giving thanks in all things" for this is the will of God in Christ Jesus. Finding our calling and fulfilling it is ultimately in God's hands. He is the author of our story, the one who calls us, and the one who will go with us as we dare to follow his call and fight the battles he leads us into. Even if it seems that we miss his cues or misunderstand, or even go in the wrong direction we can be confident that God is with us and will guide us if we continue to seek him and willingly obey what we already know of his will as revealed in the Bible. (I don't think we should expect God to give personal revelation if we refuse to follow the sacred revelation already given in the Bible.) However, even though we may get off track sometimes and misunderstand, I don't think we should worry that we will miss God's call, because it is God who sends the call. He will also complete each of our stories as we respond.

In *The Silver Chair,* Jill Pole and Eustace Scrubb are called into Narnia to rescue Prince Rilian from the enchantment which held him captive. Upon arriving, Jill receives several specific signs from Aslan, which she and Eustace were to follow to find the prince. However, in the course of their journey, through their own errors and mistakes, they misread or entirely miss several of the signs. But they trust in Aslan, seek to do good and try to be faithful while making their way along in strange lands. They commit their way to his care, and follow their guide, Puddleglum the Marsh-wiggle. They still miss almost all the signs and fear for their lives when the Giants of Harfang add them to the menu for their autumnal feast! They escape and hope for Aslan's protection.

In the end, they rescue the prince, kill the evil snake and fulfill their calling by trusting Aslan and obeying the last sign. This gives me great hope: even when we aren't good at understanding the call or following the way, by God's grace we can still fulfill our calling. Philippians 1:6 gives us this assurance: "He who has begun a good work in you will complete it until the day of Jesus Christ."

A CALLING TO A SPECIFIC TASK AT A SPECIFIC TIME
There's another type of calling, where a person is impressed by God to

go a certain place or do a certain good thing. This was the case when a disciple named Philip preached Christ to the Samaritans shortly after Jesus had ascended back into heaven. Philip played a significant role in a great act of God (described in Acts 8). Then, while Philip went about his preaching ministry, he received a specific call. An angel of the Lord spoke to him, with specific directions: "Arise and go toward the south along the road which goes down from Jerusalem to Gaza."

The angel didn't say why, to whom Philip would speak, or what he was to do. He was just told to go, so he went. Given the happenings at the time, he was probably expecting an adventure. This road made its way from the capital of Jerusalem south through Gaza (our present-day Gaza strip) and on down into Egypt and all Africa. A very influential man was traveling that road, having come to Jerusalem to seek God. God had a larger plan to have that man, an official for the Queen of the Ethiopians, take the gospel to his continent. But all Philip knew was what the angel had said: get up and go.

When Philip arrived at the busy thoroughfare, he observed a man in his chariot reading aloud from the book of Isaiah. The Spirit prompted Philip, saying to him, "Go near and overtake this chariot." So he did. Hearing what the man was reading, Philip asked if he understood it, and the man asked how he could unless someone explained it to him. Philip led the man to believe that Jesus Christ is the Son of God who fulfilled Isaiah's prophecy. Immediately, seeing water nearby, the man asked to be baptized, so Philip baptized him. When the man came up from the water, Philip had disappeared! The Bible says, "The Spirit of the Lord caught Philip away," and he was found at Azotus, which is about twenty miles away. (In Harry Potter's world that would be called apperating!) The Ethiopian official came up out of the water and went on his way rejoicing!

Talk about an adventure, all because Philip was responsive to the prompting of the Holy Spirit. In situations where you have an idea of something good you could do or some way you could help resist evil, or have a desire to go a certain place—if it is within God's moral will as revealed in the Bible, and there is nothing to be lost or no harm from following such an impression, it doesn't hurt to follow it. The Bible tells us that Jesus went about doing good and overcoming the works of the devil. Anywhere there was good that he could do, he did it. Anywhere he saw a chance to defeat the devil in someone's life, he did it. So when Jesus said, "Come, follow me," he was calling us to go about doing good and fighting evil.

Our call is a call to action, not to learn religious sayings or just to think kind thoughts. Jesus wasn't impressed with people who just heard his words but didn't live by them. He called such people foolish and predicted that all they build in life would collapse. However, Jesus said that those who heard his word and took obedient action were wise. When the storms of life would come, as they come to all, their lives would not collapse. I see our call to follow Jesus as a call to join him in taking action against evil and for good.

For example, it's one thing to hear someone speak about abortion and think that is a terrible practice; it's another thing to take in a young woman who is pregnant and give her the support she needs to get through the pregnancy. It's one thing to feel sorry for a person lacking food or clothing or shelter. It's another to answer the call to help in some tangible way.

God will use whoever is willing to answer his call. We, like our heroes, may feel hesitant. We may balk at the call or doubt we can carry out his commands. We may get confused and lose our way. However, if we are to experience the fullness of life God intends we must heed his call and cross the threshold into the extraordinary. That's our next chapter.

3

Crossing the Threshold into the Extraordinary

"He could not return to living full-time with the Dursleys, not now that he knew the other world, the one to which he really belonged."

Harry Potter, Harry Potter and the Order of the Phoenix

There comes a point in every fantastic story where the hero crosses the threshold into the extraordinary world, where the battle between good and evil was already under way. This usually requires a decision, a choice to commit oneself to the adventure. In *The Magician's Nephew* Digory and Polly stumble into the secret study of Uncle Andrew, a self-proclaimed magician who holds himself above the rules of common decency that bind lesser beings. Not wanting to risk such an adventure himself, he wants to send someone else into another world, someone who could come back and tell him about it. He has been hoping to use two children in his experiments. He locks them in the study and begins to flatter Polly, drawing her attention to four bright rings—two yellow, two green—on the table. He offers her a yellow one, and she reaches out to take it before Digory can warn her against it. The moment she touches it, she disappears.

Digory demands to know how Polly will get back. The green rings remaining on the table, Uncle Andrew explains, can bring her back. Digory has a choice to make: he can put the green rings in his pocket and touch the yellow ring, taking whatever adventure and attendant dangers would await him in another world; or he could refuse to cross over. Digory chooses to go rescue Polly. He takes a step of faith and crosses the threshold into the extraordinary.

Luke Skywalker's other world is the battle against the Empire. When he chooses to go to Alderon with Obi-Wan Kenobi to deliver the plans hidden in R2-D2, he crosses the threshold into an extraordinary adventure, joining the rebellion and beginning his journey to becoming a Jedi Knight. In doing so, he experiences the invisible, supernatural powers of the Force—practicing using his Light Saber with a helmet covering his eyes, seeing that which is unseen.

There are several portals into Harry Potter's extraordinary world: the wall behind the Leaky Cauldron that opens to Diagon Alley, the barrier between platforms nine and ten at King's Cross station that offers access to Platform 9 3/4 and the Hogwarts Express, the Knight Bus that picks up stranded wizards wherever they are in need, whether in the muggle or magical worlds, fireplaces connected to the floo network and ordinary objects that are—unbeknownst to muggles—portkeys.

In some cases, characters are thrust across the threshold into the extraordinary world without their consent. In *The Voyage of the "Dawn Treader,"* Eustace Scrubb is drawn into Narnia through the painting of the Narnian ship while with his cousins, Lucy and Edmund, who'd been to Narnia before. He had no choice about it; his only choice was how to react or respond to the adventure.

Whether the character likes it or not—crossing the threshold into the extraordinary is a point of commitment. The limits of the ordinary world are suspended; new creatures, new rules and a new array of powerful forces must be faced.

Advantages of an Extraordinary World

C. S. Lewis defended his fantasy writings by stating, "A child's longing for fairy land is very different [from his interest in school stories or 're-alistic' fiction]. Does anyone," he asks,

> suppose that he really and prosaically longs for all the dangers and discomforts of a fairy tale . . . really wants dragons in contempo-rary England? . . . It would be much truer to say that fairy land arouses a longing for he knows not what. It stirs and troubles him (to his lifelong enrichment) with the dim sense of something be-yond his reach and, far from dulling or emptying the actual world, gives it a new dimension of depth. He does not despise real woods because he has read of enchanted woods: the reading makes all real woods a little enchanted.[1]

Writers choose the form of a fantastic story or fairy tale because it allows the reader to experience the wonder of supernatural worlds. Lewis wrote "fairy tales" for adults and children because he believed that "fairy tales liberate archetypes which dwell in the collective un-conscious, and when we read a good fairy tale, we are obeying the old precept, 'Know Thyself.'"[2] An essay on fantasy in *Reading the Classics with C. S. Lewis* explains what Lewis saw as the advantages of using ex-traordinary worlds:

> In the same way reading about enchanted woods confers a sense of enchantment and wonder on real woods, so too does reading about "enchanted religion" deepen the sense of awe and wonder, and indeed the significance and meaning, of religion in this world. Lewis believed that Christianity is the poorer for its lack of a sense of wonder, and responses to it can be paralyzed by the demands it makes for suitably reverential attitudes and emotions. . . . The sus-tained response to the Narnian Chronicles has proven that Lewis's

theory was correct. Additionally, it is clear that the genre of fantasy offered Lewis the greatest opportunities for creating literary works of enduring power.[3]

Lewis saw that a fantasy story lets the reader pass by dutiful religious ritual to experience the truths fully, without muting the emotional experience:

> The whole subject [religion] was associated with lowered voices, almost as if it were something medical. But supposing that by casting all these things into an imaginary world, stripping them of their stained-glass and Sunday school associations, one could make them for the first time appear in their real potency? Could one not thus steal past those watchful dragons? I thought one could.[4]

WHEN ORDINARY AND EXTRAORDINARY WORLDS CONVERGE

I find one of the most interesting aspects of the Harry Potter series to be how ordinary and extraordinary worlds converge. The muggle and magical worlds operate pretty much separately; we see, however, that the magical world influences the muggle world, and there are places like the Leaky Cauldron and Kings Cross Station where the worlds directly interact continually. While there are portals between the worlds, one must have knowledge, acceptance and confidence to pass from the ordinary world into the extraordinary. The Dursleys see Harry go through the barrier between platform's nine and ten at Kings Cross, but they never pass through the barrier because they don't believe in such nonsense. Some muggles do believe and accept the magical world, however, and they manage to get into the wizarding world. Hermione's parents—both muggles—are with her in Diagon Alley, where they met the Weasleys.

Those in the extraordinary world also have the ability to cross over into the ordinary world. Professors Dumbledore and McGonagall arrive on Privet Drive to deliver the baby Harry to his blood relatives. Mrs. Figg, a squib from the wizarding world, is a long-term plant in Harry's neighborhood, and Mundungus Fletcher is sent there to keep an eye on him. Dementors show up in Little Whining, and damage caused by rampaging giants is blamed on a hurricane. The Minister of Magic appears in the office of the newly appointed Prime Minister of Britain and is given the moniker "The Other Minister." He is announced through a magical painting, and arrives via floo powder to update the Prime Minister on happenings in the wizarding world that affect his world whenever the severity of the situation warrants a visit.

This interplay between our world and other worlds is also seen in the Chronicles of Narnia. In *The Magician's Nephew* Jadis, former Queen of Charn, is loosed on the streets of London, where she commandeers a hansom cab and rips the bar off a lamp post. This piece of iron from our world later grows into the lamp post of Lantern Waste in Narnia, where Jadis throws it during Narnia's creation. Jadis wreaks havoc all over London as she plots to make herself queen of our world, but thankfully she is dragged back into the Wood between the Worlds.

In this and several other instances we see significant interaction between extraordinary worlds and our ordinary world. What a fantastic illustration of the interaction between the invisible supernatural realm and our material realm depicted in the Bible. Our physical world, we are led to understand, is surrounded and influenced by an unseen spiritual world.

In the Bible we see angels being sent as messengers from one realm to the other. We see that spiritual battles taking place in the "heavenly realms" delay answers to prayer in our world. This was the case when Daniel was praying to understand a vision. In Daniel 10:10-14 we learn that an angel—who shows up three weeks after he started out to deliver God's answer to Daniel's prayer—has been detained by the "prince of Persia." Apparently a spiritual force of evil with authority over Persia battled him so fiercely that it took time to get past him.

We see appearances of "the Lord" in the Old Testament, and in the New Testament we hear from Paul the apostle that he was "caught up into the third heaven." Angels appear at Christ's tomb, accompanied by an earthquake. Throughout the Bible, we see an assumption that there is an extraordinary world, unseen and unrealized by most "muggles"—or people who have not crossed the threshold into the extraordinary. This extraordinary, supernatural world directly influences our lives, whether people recognize it or not.

FOR THOSE WHO HAVE EYES TO SEE

Crossing over into the extraordinary world sometimes requires an ability to see "by faith" that which is unseen or what some cannot see. In *The Lion, the Witch and the Wardrobe* Lucy is able to go directly into Narnia through the wardrobe and see the snowy woods the first time. Peter, Susan and Edmund look into the wardrobe at Lucy's urging and can't see anything extraordinary. In *Prince Caspian* Lucy can see Aslan when he appears to lead them to the meeting place, but he is invisible to the others. It is only after they start following the invisible Aslan, at Lucy's insistence, that he begins to appear to all, even Trumpkin the skeptical dwarf.

In the Harry Potter stories one also has to have "eyes to see." Consider Harry's first approach to the Leaky Cauldron:

> "This is it," said Hagrid, coming to a halt, "The Leaky Cauldron. It's a famous place." It was a tiny, grubby-looking pub. If Hagrid hadn't pointed it out, Harry wouldn't have noticed it was there. The people hurrying by didn't glance at it. Their eyes slid from the big book shop on one side to the record shop on the other as if they couldn't see the Leaky Cauldron at all. In fact, Harry had the most peculiar feeling that only he and Hagrid could see it. Before he could mention this Hagrid had steered him inside.

The headquarters for the Order of the Phoenix at 12 Grinnauld Place, the phone booth entry to the Ministry of Magic and St. Mungo's Hospital all have points of entry in the ordinary world but may or may not be noticed by muggles. As Jesus said repeatedly, some things are "for those who have eyes to see . . ."

EXTRAORDINARY CREATURES

What fantasy story would be complete without fantastic beasts and extraordinary creatures? The world of Harry Potter is populated with classic creatures and beasts of fairytale, folklore, legend and myth, plus a few that J. K. Rowling created for good measure.[5] Narnia is populated with fantastic creatures of medieval folklore and myth. Lewis suggested that "the psychological awakening achieved through archetypal images and patterns in literature may also be provoked by the use in such stories of non-human characters, such as dwarf, giants and talking beasts."[6] *Star Wars* films have Wookiees, Ewoks and all manner of creatures alien to us, both good and evil.

The spiritual realm into which the Bible allows us to glimpse is also populated with extraordinary creatures, spirits and beings. These include angels (ministering spirits sent to serve those who will inherit salvation), fallen angels or demons, spirits of the dead, evil spirits, deceiving spirits, lying spirits, and spirits of demons that perform miraculous signs. There's even a behemoth and leviathan (a gliding serpent or sea monster), a dragon, a talking serpent, a girl who can foretell the future, cherubim, seraphs with six wings, and one talking donkey! Our awareness of otherworldly creatures and spirits gives depth to a view that life spans natural and supernatural realms.

BIBLE STORIES OF CROSSING THE THRESHOLD

For the most part, each person has to make a decision to step over into the spiritual realm. Although there are a few cases where God showed up whether or not the person was ready, crossing the threshold is a memorable part of many grand stories in the Bible.

No turning back. Even though a person who crosses the threshold may be able to go back where they came from, their life can never go back to normal. Elisha was a young man from a wealthy family. One day he was plowing his father's fields, driving a pair of oxen along with eleven other oxen teams. He saw the prophet Elijah, a man renowned for many miracles, who approached and threw his cloak around the younger man's shoulders. This gesture was a call to Elisha to join him in the extraordinary life of the prophets. Elisha didn't just say goodbye to his family; he made his decision final! He broke the wooden yoke holding his oxen together, slaughtered his oxen, and used the wood from the broken yoke for a sacrificial fire to burn them on. He went on to perform and witness many miracles in the Lord's power and transverse between natural and supernatural realms.

Unwilling entrance to the extraordinary world. The extraordinary world broke into the ordinary life of a Babylonian king unbidden, though not unprovoked:

> King Belshazzar gave a great banquet for a thousand of his nobles and drank wine with them. While Belshazzar was drinking his wine, he gave orders to bring in the gold and silver goblets that Nebuchadnezzar his father had taken from the temple in Jerusalem, so that the king and his nobles, his wives and his concubines might drink from them. So they brought in the gold goblets that had been taken from the temple of God in Jerusalem, and the king and his nobles, his wives and his concubines drank from them. As they drank the wine, they praised the gods of gold and silver, of bronze, iron, wood and stone. (Daniel 5:1-4)

This turned out to be a *very* bad idea. Apparently God doesn't take kindly to people desecrating holy items stolen from his temple while praising the elements they were made from instead of the Creator who made everything. It was time for the ordinary and extraordinary worlds to converge visibly.

> Suddenly the fingers of a human hand appeared and wrote on the plaster of the wall, near the lampstand in the royal palace. The king watched the hand as it wrote. His face turned pale and he was so frightened that his knees knocked together and his legs gave way. (Daniel 5:5-6)

Being unfamiliar with the language etched in his wall, the king needed help from someone who had more experience with the extraordinary world.

> The king called out for the enchanters, astrologers and diviners to be brought and said to these wise men of Babylon, "Whoever reads this writing and tells me what it means will be clothed in purple and have a gold chain placed around his neck, and he will be made the third highest ruler in the kingdom."
>
> Then all the king's wise men came in, but they could not read the writing or tell the king what it meant. So King Belshazzar became even more terrified and his face grew more pale. His nobles were baffled. (Daniel 5:7-9)

Where does a guy turn when he's in trouble? It's Mom to the rescue. The Queen Mother had been around long enough to know there was someone who had a connection with God, who had helped the previous king when his magicians, astrologers, and diviners failed him too.

> The queen, hearing the voices of the king and his nobles, came into the banquet hall. "O king, live forever!" she said. "Don't be alarmed! Don't look so pale! There is a man in your kingdom who has the spirit of the holy gods in him. In the time of your father he was found to have insight and intelligence and wisdom like that of

the gods. King Nebuchadnezzar your father—your father the king, I say—appointed him chief of the magicians, enchanters, astrologers and diviners. This man Daniel, whom the king called Belteshazzar, was found to have a keen mind and knowledge and understanding, and also the ability to interpret dreams, explain riddles and solve difficult problems. Call for Daniel, and he will tell you what the writing means."

So Daniel was brought before the king, and the king said to him, "Are you Daniel, one of the exiles my father the king brought from Judah? I have heard that the spirit of the gods is in you and that you have insight, intelligence and outstanding wisdom. The wise men and enchanters were brought before me to read this writing and tell me what it means, but they could not explain it. Now I have heard that you are able to give interpretations and to solve difficult problems. If you can read this writing and tell me what it means, you will be clothed in purple and have a gold chain placed around your neck, and you will be made the third highest ruler in the kingdom."

Then Daniel answered the king, "You may keep your gifts for yourself and give your rewards to someone else. Nevertheless, I will read the writing for the king and tell him what it means." (Daniel 5:11-17)

Daniel went on to tell him that God was about to give his kingdom to the Medes and the Persians. And, as we know from biblical and secular historical records, that's precisely what happened. So in his case the extraordinary world broke into the natural world to deliver the just deserts that evil king deserved!

For those who have eyes to see. Some characters in fantasy stories can see things others cannot; this is a recurrent aspect of God's kingdom in our world as well. Elisha the prophet lived when Israel was at war with

Aram. The king of Israel had a distinct advantage because God kept giving away national security secrets and military strategy to Elisha.

The king of Aram summoned his officers. "Which of us is on the side of the king of Israel?"

One of his officers responded, "Elisha, the prophet who is in Israel, tells the king of Israel the very words you speak in your bedroom."

So he sent to have Elisha arrested. When the troops arrived, Elisha's servant saw an army with horses and chariots had surrounded the city. "Oh, my lord, what shall we do?"

"Don't be afraid," the prophet told him. "Those who are with us are more than those who are with them."

What did he mean? We have to pity the servant of Elisha; all he could see were armies of the king of Aram arrayed against them. Elisha saw something very different because he could see the heavenly realm. Elisha prayed, "O LORD, open his eyes so he may see." Then the servant's eyes were opened to the extraordinary spiritual realm surrounding the ordinary. He could now see the previously invisible armies of heaven God had sent to fight on their behalf. That made all the difference. (See 2 Kings 6:9-23 for the whole story.)

Perhaps Elisha didn't have to have extraordinary faith. Perhaps he could already see the heavenly realm as clearly as we see the earthly one, and simply had to act accordingly.

When ordinary and extraordinary worlds converge in the Bible. Jacob crossed the threshold into the extraordinary when he saw a stairway between earth and heaven with angels ascending and descending. The Hebrews saw the fire of God on the holy mountain when Moses received the Law. Elisha watched as Elijah was taken up to heaven in a chariot of fire. Peter, James, and John saw Jesus transfigured before them; a bright cloud enveloped them, and they heard a voice from the cloud said, "This is my Son, whom I love; with him I am well pleased. Listen to him!" They saw Jesus speaking with Moses and Elijah. Their world had intersected the world of ancient history, seeing the giver of the Law and the premier prophet of God. They caught a glimpse of heavenly glory—on earth. These and others whose stories are related to us in the Bible crossed way over into the extraordinary and the supernatural burst into their ordinary world. The kingdom of heaven had come and converged with their ordinary world. There was no going back after that!

Human beings long for the supernatural, even though we also fear it. We sense another realm beyond this one and want to know more about it. Some people seek to find it through various means the Bible says are dangerous and wrong, like séances or mediums. Others seek God and ask him to reveal himself in supernatural ways. Some simply rely on fantastic stories which allow us to imagine life beyond the limitations of our ordinary world. Spiritually speaking, people long for more than a religion of rules; we want an experience of wonder, awe, supernatural experiences. We want a glimpse into the worlds beyond our own. I believe this desire is in us because God created us to live in personal relationship with himself, even though he cannot be contained in our ordinary world. As we consider the quest of our stories, let us not neglect our personal quest to cross over into the extraordinary in our own lives too. There we will find ourselves in the midst of a cosmic battle between good and evil. We will need our mentor to help us find and take up our place in that battle. We will look at the meeting with the mentor in our next chapter.

4

Meeting with the Mentor

"And the things you have heard me say in the presence of many witnesses entrust to reliable men who will also be qualified to teach others."

Apostle Paul to Timothy (2 Timothy 2:2)

The Mentor is typically the wise old man or woman who takes on the role of protector, guide, revealer, teacher, motivator and coach for the hero. In any story, various characters can play the role of a mentor, but there is usually someone designated as the primary mentor in the story. In *Star Wars: A New Hope,* Luke's primary mentor is Obi-Wan Kenobi, who had been a mentor to his father before him. Later, Yoda will become Luke's primary mentor, as he had been to Obi-Wan Kenobi. In Narnia, Aslan is the primary mentor, although the children find other mentors when Aslan is not present, like Mr. and Mrs. Beaver in *The Lion, the Witch and the Wardrobe*, Puddleglum the Marsh-wiggle in *The Silver Chair,* and Dr. Cornelius in *Prince Caspian*. Harry Potter's primary mentor is Albus Dumbledore, although all the teachers play mentoring roles to varying degrees.

The role of the mentor is to help the hero prepare for his battles and challenges, to overcome doubts and fears, provide motivation, insight and knowledge that will be needed to complete the hero's journey and defeat the evil foe. Mentors help heroes figure out the meaning of what they're going through and keep them moving in the right direction while developing their skills.

Sometimes the role of the mentor can be carried on and supplemented by an inner voice or code of conduct the hero carries with him, helping distinguish right from wrong, good from evil. This is the case in *Star Wars: A New Hope,* when Luke Skywalker takes his X-wing fighter into the Death Star, with the fate of many worlds dependent on his shot hitting the mark. He hears the voice of his mentor telling him to trust the Force. Although Obi-Wan is no longer with him in life, he has left his message imprinted on Luke's consciousness and is thus able to speak to him from the spirit realm. Being a Jedi in training, Luke would judge his decisions and his conduct according to the Jedi Code.

Harry Potter's mentor Dumbledore tells him that he would never truly leave Hogwarts as long as some there were loyal to him, and help would always come to those who asked. So when Harry is cornered in the Chamber of Secrets, he remains loyal to his mentor and calls out for help, which proves to be his salvation in that situation.

How similar is this to Jesus' promise to his followers: he will be with us always, even until the end of the age, and wherever two or three gather in his name he is in the midst of them? We have God's Word, which we can memorize and carry internally. We have the Holy Spirit indwelling us to help us call these to mind and apply them in the midst of our battles. We also have human mentors who—hopefully—live out a biblical code of conduct, encourage and guide us.

A ROLE MODEL WORTHY OF THE HERO'S ASPIRATIONS

Those playing the role of mentor model the hero's aspirations. Often they are former heroes who now want to pass on their mantle of wisdom and knowledge to help ensure the success of their cause. In *The Lion, the Witch and the Wardrobe*, Aslan is the primary mentor, but those who have gone before pass on their knowledge and faith to those who enter Narnia after them. Susan and Peter go to old Professor Kirke with their worries about Lucy's reported experience in the wardrobe. He acts as a mentor to them, encouraging them to open themselves to the possibility that Lucy might be telling the truth. He is a worthy mentor, we learn in *The Magician's Nephew*, because this old professor had been the boy Digory and had gone to Narnia before them.

Obi-Wan Kenobi is a great Jedi warrior, trained by Yoda and Qui-Gon Jinn. He goes on to train Anakin Skywalker, then—many years later—trains Luke. In the Harry Potter stories, Dumbledore is a mentor worthy of admiration and devotion. He is calm, courageous, protective of Harry, devoted to goodness, and committed to fighting evil, even to the point of self-sacrifice.

The ideal mentor in spiritual life is much like an excellent mentor in a fantastic story. You want someone whose life is further along on the path you are following. You don't just want someone who can talk a good game. You want someone who is willing to hold up his life as well as his instruction for assessment. The writer of the letter to the Hebrews instructs his readers: "Remember your leaders, who spoke the word of God to you. Consider the outcome of their way of life and imitate their faith" (Hebrews 13:7). Paul also instructs Timothy, the young pastor he mentored, to let his life be worthy of admiration and imitation. He tells him, "Don't let anyone look down on you because you are young, but set an example for the believers in speech, in life, in love, in faith and in purity" (1 Timothy 4:12). It's not just about what mentors have to say, even if it comes from God; their way of life and observable faith is important.

MEETING WITH THE MENTOR

Once the hero crosses over into the extraordinary world of his adventure, it won't be long before the initial meeting with the mentor. Mentors are often used by the author to introduce the character to the new world, explain what is expected, what rules must be followed and how things are to proceed. In Narnia, Mr. and Mrs. Beaver instruct Peter, Susan, Edmund and Lucy. In *Prince Caspian* the old nurse and later Dr. Cornelius serve as initial mentors. However, eventually in every Narnian story, the children encounter their greatest mentor, Aslan himself.

The meeting with the mentor can serve several purposes. In *Star Wars: A New Hope,* Luke's first mentor, Obi-Wan Kenobi, also acts as a herald. Their first meeting is monumental, calling Luke into the battle against the evil Empire. Obi-Wan's call for Luke to go with him to Alderon sets the course for his entire future.

Meeting with the mentor can also be a time of testing, as the mentor sizes up the student. When Luke first meets Yoda, in *Star Wars: The Empire Strikes Back,* he doesn't realize that the wrinkled little fellow testing his patience after he crashed into the swamp is his future mentor.

Luke says, "R2, what are we doing here? It's like something out of a dream. Maybe I'm just going crazy. Now all I've got to do is find this Yoda, if he even exists." A small wrinkled creature appears in the mist.

Luke says, "I am looking for someone."

"Looking? Found someone you have." Yoda continues, "Help you, I can, yes."

Luke says, "I don't think so, I am looking for a great warrior."

Yoda laughs this off saying, "Wars not make one great . . ." while taking a bite of Luke's food. Yoda—his identity still unknown to Luke—rifles through his tool chest extracting a small lamp. When Luke and R2-D2 try to retrieve it, Yoda threatens not to help.

"I don't want your help," says Luke. "I want my lamp back."

All the while his future mentor is sizing him up as he complains about wanting to get his ship out of this "slimy mud-hole" which Yoda calls home.

Yoda tells Luke, "I am your friend."

"I'm not looking for a friend. I am looking for a Jedi Master."

"You're looking for Yoda. I will take you to him," says Yoda.

Yoda then insists that Luke eat with him. While eating, he asks Luke, "Why must you become a Jedi?"

"Mostly because of my father, I guess."

Yoda responds, "Father, powerful Jedi was he. Mmm . . . powerful Jedi."

Luke replies, "How could you know my father? I don't even know what I'm doing here. I don't have time for this."

Yoda then pronounces, "I cannot teach him. The boy has no patience."

Obi-Wan Kenobi's voice is heard, "He will learn patience."

Yoda says to Obi-Wan, "Much anger in him, like his father."

"Was I any different when you taught me?" asks Obi-Wan.

Yoda declares, "No, he is not ready."

Finally Luke catches on—now pleading. "Yoda! I am ready. I . . . Ben . . . I can be a Jedi. Ben, tell him. I am ready."

"Ready, are you?" Yoda asks, indignantly. "What know you . . . ready? For eight hundred years have I trained Jedi. My own counsel will I keep on who is to be trained. A Jedi must have the deepest commitment, the most serious mind. This one a long time I have watched. All his life, as he looked away to the future, to the horizon. Never his mind on where he was; what he was doing. Adventure! Hah! Excitement! Humph! A Jedi craves not these things. You are reckless!"

Obi-Wan interjects, "So was I, if you remember."

"He is too old. Yes, too old to begin the training."

Luke pleads, "But I've learned so much . . ."

Luke's meeting with Yoda and Yoda's acceptance of him as an apprentice changes, even brings about, Luke's destiny and that of the entire galaxy. First, however, the mentor has to examine his potential apprentice.

Harry Potter's first meeting with his mentor, Albus Dumbledore, takes place on the night he becomes known as "the boy who lived," the night

Dumbledore takes him to live with his mother's sister and her family. This sets the course for Harry's life and may have saved his life by protecting him from Voldemort. Once at Hogwarts, Harry meets Dumbledore as his headmaster. Every year, Harry's meeting with his mentor teaches him more about his history and destiny.

HISTORY AND DESTINY

Mentors often know more about the hero's history and destiny than the hero does. Obi-Wan and Yoda know that Luke and Leia are twins, children of Anakin and Padmé Skywalker. They know details of their birth and upbringing still secret to the heroes. They also know about the prophecy Anakin was appointed to fulfill. This knowledge gives the mentors a fondness for the heroes and motivation to train them.

The prophecy about Harry Potter and Voldemort was given to Dumbledore. He has to decide how much to reveal to Harry and at what rate. Toward the end of each year, after Harry has faced his challenges and fought his battles, Dumbledore explains the meaning of things to Harry. Harry's back story and future destiny are revealed in these meetings. As Harry gets further along in his training, Dumbledore's training becomes overt; in Harry's sixth year, Dumbledore tries to teach Harry all he needs to know to fulfill his purpose and destroy Voldemort.

THE MENTOR AS FORCE OF CONSCIENCE, TEACHER AND COACH

The mentor often acts as the hero's conscience. In *The Voyage of the "Dawn Treader"* Lucy is supposed to be finding a spell to make Duffers visible. Aslan growls at her for instead using spells in the magician's book to make herself prettier and for eavesdropping on her friends gossiping about her. When Aslan's face appears in the pages of the magic book, she accepts his reprimand and moves on to the spell she was sent there to use.

Dumbledore is a force of conscience—by virtue of Harry Potter's intense desire to please him. All it takes is a twitch of Dumbledore's moustache when mentioning that Harry has "a certain disregard for rules" to make Harry remorseful. When Harry uses the Marauder's Map to sneak out of Hogwarts and into Hogsmead without permission he is chastised by Professor Lupin, a secondary mentor whose words of disappointment were more effective than detention at pricking Harry's conscience.

When Luke has finally advanced to being mentored by Yoda, Yoda is intent on teaching him what he must know to become a Jedi Knight. But Luke is distracted. Luke tries to raise his swamped ship, with Yoda offering instruction: "Use the Force! Concentrate!"

Luke says, "We'll never get it out now."

"So certain are you," says Yoda, telling him he must unlearn what he previously learned. Luke whines that he is trying, to which Yoda replied, "No, try not. Do or do not. There is no try."

"I can't. It is too big," says Luke.

"Size matters not. Look at me. Judge me by my size, do you?" The mentor then teaches by doing; Yoda raises the ship out of the swamp using the Force. In amazement, Luke exclaims, "I don't believe it!"

Yoda replies, "That is why you fail." Precious lessons!

HELP IN THE QUEST

In fantastic stories, the mentor can plant information or helpful props that the hero will need to complete the quest. The mentor also pushes the character to learn what will be needed to complete the journey. In *Harry Potter and the Sorcerer's Stone* Dumbledore anonymously gives Harry his father's invisibility cloak with the note, "Use it well." Harry uses the cloak to explore the school and runs across the Mirror of Erised. Dumbledore finds Harry gazing into the mirror, which shows him his heart's desire, and teaches him how the mirror works. Only in the climactic show-down between Harry and Professor Quirrell does Harry realize that Dumbledore arranged for him to learn all he needed to succeed; the Sorcerer's Stone could be retrieved out of the mirror only by one who wanted to *retrieve it,* not by one who wanted to *use* it. Harry has the right idea when he says of his mentor:

> He's a funny man, Dumbledore. . . . I think he knows more or less everything that goes on here, you know. I reckon he had a pretty good idea we were going to try, and instead of stopping us, he just taught us enough to help. I don't think it was an accident he let me find out how the mirror worked. It's almost like he thought I had the right to face Voldemort if I could.

Harry's mentor gives him the knowledge and opportunities needed to fight his battle. Harry still has free will; he chooses to go through the trap door and try to retrieve the Sorcerer's Stone to protect Hogwarts. However, there is someone watching over him who helps him along.

Just as in literature there is a recurrent paradox between the knowledge—even foreknowledge—of the mentor and the choices of the apprentice, a paradoxical relationship exists in Scripture between predestination and free will. Luke Skywalker wrestles back and forth between trusting his own voice and the voice of his mentors. He has not only his own thoughts to lead him but also the voices of his mentors Yoda and Obi-Wan Kenobi. When Luke masters the Force enough to see a dangerous future for his friends Han Solo and Leia, Yoda tries to persuade him to finish his training before he leaves, but ultimately concedes as Luke leaves Dagobah. This reminds me of how we sometimes wrestle between walking in the flesh and walking in the Spirit, listening to our own counsel, that of our earthly mentors and the voice of the Holy Spirit. The Holy Spirit instructs us in God's word, encourages us to do the right things and yet allows us to exercise free will in our service of God.

THE MENTOR IN DISGUISE OR INVISIBLE

We get the sense in fantasy stories that one never really knows when a mentor may show up, when the hero is being observed or being helped by the mentor. In *The Voyage of the "Dawn Treader,"* Lucy is coerced into uttering the incantation to make invisible things visible again. Suddenly there in the doorway, warm, solid and fully present, stands Aslan. Lucy thanks him for coming, to which he replies, "I have been here all the time, but you have just made me visible."

The mentors in the *Star Wars* series seem to appear when needed most. Obi-Wan watches and hears Yoda test Luke, invisible to Luke until he joins the conversation. In *Harry Potter and the Sorcerer's Stone* Harry returns to gaze again into the Mirror of Erised and notices Dumbledore in the room. When questioned, Dumbledore notes that some wizards don't require an invisibility cloak to be invisible, inferring that he had been there all along.

Another example of the mentor being present without the hero real- izing it or recognizing him occurs in *The Horse and His Boy*. Shasta is sep- arated from his companions, alone at night in the tombs. He is fright- ened, but comforted by a cat that comes to stay with him. He doesn't realize until later that the cat was really Aslan in another form. In that same story, Shasta and Aravis are riding their horses and being chased by what seems to them several lions. They speed up considerably, as if riding for their lives, and make it across the drawbridge in the nick of time. At the end of the story, Aslan reveals that there were not many lions or cats; there was only one, him. He was the cat in the tombs with Shasta and the one who hurried them along to get to safety. Their mentor was with them when they didn't know it.

Mentors may actually cause affliction and adversity to teach and guide us. Aslan scratches Aravis painfully while hurrying her along through the desert in *The Horse and His Boy*. Yoda requires Luke to endure a rig- orous training program. In Harry's fourth year, Dumbledore allows him to face the dangers and extreme challenges of the Triwizard Tournament.

We might be staggered to think that some experiences that are painful or frightening, or that cause us to get moving, may be our mentor in disguise. The prophet Isaiah reveals this, explaining,

> Although the Lord gives you the bread of adversity and the water of affliction, your teachers will be hidden no more; with your own eyes you will see them. Whether you turn to the right or to the left, your ears will hear a voice behind you, saying, "This is the way; walk in it." (Isaiah 30:20-21)

So we are reminded that the Holy Spirit, as our invisible mentor, is always with us even when we don't recognize God's presence.

PASS IT ON!

As the time comes for the student to go to the next level, he or she may see one mentor replace another, or grow to be a mentor themselves instead of just an apprentice. The role of mentor is passed on in hopes that one day the apprentice will become mentor to another. Luke Skywalker is first trained by Obi-Wan Kenobi, then must move on to Yoda according to Obi-Wan's prophecy on Hoth. When Yoda dies, Luke doesn't stop growing. He doesn't have Yoda and Obi-Wan with him, but he remembers their instruction and listens to the internalized Jedi Code and voices of his former mentors from the spirit realm.

Since it is the mentor's job to propel the hero toward his or her destiny, there usually comes a time when the mentor steps back and allows the hero or hero team to proceed on their own, using all they have learned. At that time the hero should also accept the mission to pass on what has been taught, by becoming a mentor to others. Consider Yoda's last conversation with Luke:

"Master Yoda, you can't die."

"Strong am I with the Force, but not that strong. Twilight is upon me and soon night must fall. That is the way of things, the way of the Force," says Yoda weakly.

"But I need your help."

"No more training you receive. Already know that which you need," Yoda replies. After some discussion of Luke's father and reminders about not giving in to the dark side, Yoda utters his final admonition to his apprentice: "Pass on what you have learned." Yoda uses his dying breath to urge Luke to pass on what his mentors had taught him.

In most good fantasy, there is a pattern of one generation mentoring a few in the next generation to carry on the fight against evil and preserve that which is good. Portraits of former headmasters and headmistresses of Hogwarts pass on advice to the current one. Dumbledore and the other teachers of his generation, trained James Potter, Lily Evans, Remus Lupin, Sirius Black, Severus Snape, and their generation, who then have a hand in mentoring Harry and his friends. By his fifth year at Hogwarts, when Harry is far enough along in his training, he begins mentoring his peers in the Defense Association/Dumbledore's Army. The plan for passing on important knowledge and skills in the fight against evil is carried on by mentoring—or, as Jesus called it, making disciples.

OUR PRIMARY SPIRITUAL MENTOR

When Jesus was on earth, he faithfully mentored his twelve disciples. As the time of his departure approached, he assured them that they would not be left alone. Jesus told his disciples, "I will pray the Father, and he will give you another Helper, that he may abide with you forever, even the Spirit of truth" (John 14:16-17).

Jesus had taught them many things in the three years they had been together, but he could not stay with them to carry on their mentoring. They needed to go on to the next phase of God's plan for their development. Jesus told them,

> These things I have spoken to you while being present with you. But the Helper, the Holy Spirit, whom the Father will send in My

name, He will teach you all things, and bring to your remembrance all things that I said to you. (John 14:25-26)

In this way, Jesus passed the torch to the Holy Spirit to carry on when the time came for him to ascend back to the Father. As members of the Trinity, Jesus incarnate and the Holy Spirit each had their role to play in the life of the disciples. Jesus knew his disciples still had battles and challenges ahead. He warned them they would be dragged before courts and give testimony, but not to worry about what to say, because their mentor—the Holy Spirit—would tell them what to say at that moment. He is able to whisper in the ear of Jesus' followers as clearly as Yoda whispered in Luke's ear.

Jedi Knights have the Jedi Code as their code of conduct. A Jedi mentor would teach their apprentice to do only that which was in keeping with the Jedi Code. Luke could recall the code and consider whether what he was thinking of doing was in keeping with it. He could hear the voice of his mentors affirming that which the code affirmed and disallowing that which the code condemned.

This works in reverse as well. One who directed an apprentice to *disobey* the Jedi Code was not a true Jedi. When Anakin Skywalker is told by Chancellor Palpatine (Darth Sidius, unbeknownst to Anakin) to kill Dooku, Anakin hesitates, saying that to do so would not be in keeping with the Jedi Code. The chancellor urges him to disregard the Jedi Code; Dooku is too dangerous. Anakin obeys the chancellor, forsakes the code he had learned from his Jedi teachers and mentors, and descended further into darkness.

The Holy Spirit teaches us the word of God, giving us the ability to understand what is written. Jesus said,

I have many things to say to you, but you cannot bear them now. However, when He, the Spirit of truth, comes He will guide you into all truth; for He will not speak on His own authority, but whatever he hears He will speak; and He will tell you things to come. (John 16:12-13)

As Luke had Obi-Wan and Yoda to teach, explain, reinforce and help him apply the Jedi Code, we have the Holy Spirit to bring God's word to life in our hearts, minds and conscience, and reinforce what we have learned from Christian teachers and mentors. The Holy Spirit brings Bible verses to mind for reproof, correction and training in righteousness. The guidance of the Holy Spirit can be spiritual, practical, even directional; think of how the apostle Paul—sailing on his missionary journey—was forbidden by the Holy Spirit to go one direction, but prompted to go another direction. When we are feeling discouraged, the Holy Spirit acts as our comforter. As we prepare for our battles and challenges, as we face doubts and fears, the Holy Spirit is present to encourage and provide motivation, insight and knowledge. The Holy Spirit guides us into all truth, helping us discern the meaning of what we're going through and keeps us moving in the right direction. It is the Holy Spirit who seals us to protect us from the evil one and keep us until the day of salvation. He acts as our invisible protector, guide, revealer, teacher, motivator and coach; in short, our primary mentor. The Holy Spirit also inspires and fills our earthly mentors, working also through them in our lives.

EMPOWERED BY OUR MENTORS

Just as Aslan gives children supernatural powers in Narnia to do what the mission requires, as Yoda and Obi-Wan reveal to Luke how to use the power of the Force, as Harry's teachers teach him how to use knowledge and wield power in their world; similarly our mentor, the Holy Spirit, comes with power so that those serving in God's kingdom can be effective witnesses of Jesus.

Jesus told his disciples, "Behold I send the Promise of my Father upon you; but tarry in Jerusalem until you are endued with power from on high" (Luke 24:49). Again after his resurrection and before his ascension, Jesus promised, "But you will receive power when the Holy Spirit comes on you; and you will be my witnesses in Jerusalem, and in all Judea and Samaria, and to the ends of the earth" (Acts 1:8).

As we undergo the training provided by the Holy Spirit, God's power should flow through our lives to complete the missions and quests God has for us. God could have used any method imaginable to make sure his message got out to the whole world. Time and time again, the Bible reveals that God chose to use mentoring as the primary means of passing on the knowledge and skills necessary for his would-be heroes to succeed.

In the Old Testament God commanded parents and grandparents to pass on his Law and teachings to their children and grandchildren in the course of everyday life.

> Hear, O Israel: The LORD our God, the LORD is one. Love the LORD your God with all your heart and with all your soul and with all your strength. These commandments that I give you today are to be upon your hearts. Impress them on your children. Talk about them when you sit at home and when you walk along the road, when you lie down and when you get up. Tie them as symbols on your hands and bind them on your foreheads. Write them on the doorframes of your houses and on your gates. (Deuteronomy 6:4-9)

In the New Testament, Jesus Christ had only three years set aside to get his message of salvation out to the entire world. By my way of thinking, it seems that it might have been better for Jesus to come to Earth in the era of mass communication, satellite broadcasting and the Internet. However, even though God could have sent Christ at any time and given him any and every means of communication, God chose mentoring. Jesus chose twelve men and poured his life into them, day after day, teaching, training, demonstrating the use of his miraculous powers, praying with them, reprimanding them and loving them. Then, as he

was leaving—as most mentors in fantastic stories do—he commanded
them to go out and mentor others. Here's the last scene before Jesus ascended back into heaven:

> Then the eleven disciples went to Galilee, to the mountain where
> Jesus had told them to go. When they saw him, they worshiped
> him; but some doubted. Then Jesus came to them and said, "All
> authority in heaven and on earth has been given to me. Therefore
> go and make disciples of all nations, baptizing them in the name
> of the Father and of the Son and of the Holy Spirit, and teaching
> them to obey everything I have commanded you. And surely I am
> with you always, to the very end of the age." (Matthew 28:16-20)

We see the mentoring model carried on throughout the New Testament. In the Book of Acts we see Saul of Tarsus confronted by the risen
Jesus, struck blind and told to wait for instructions. God chose as Saul's
mentor a man named Ananias. God told Ananias to go to Saul, pray for
him, restore his sight and get him started following Jesus. He reluctantly
agreed, fearing that Saul was not a true believer. Later a man called Barnabas (which means "encourager" or "Son of Encouragement" [Acts 4:36])
became Saul's friend and mentor. After some years, this same man, by then
called by his Roman name, Paul, began mentoring others, including the
young man Timothy. As Paul approached death, he commanded Timothy
to become a mentor to others who would go on to mentor others.

> You then, my son, be strong in the grace that is in Christ Jesus. And
> the things you have heard me say in the presence of many wit-
> nesses entrust to reliable men who will also be qualified to teach
> others. (2 Timothy 2:1-3)

Throughout church history mentoring has been the basic model for
raising up Christian heroes to take their place in the ongoing battles
against evil.

KNOWING THE MENTOR'S VOICE

Jesus said that his sheep *know his voice* and follow him. Every Christian must learn to distinguish the voice of the Holy Spirit from other voices seeking to influence us. So, how can we be sure to be responsive to the voice of God, while ignoring or resisting other voices that would lead us astray? For example, I have heard Christians try to justify divorcing their faithful Christian spouse in order to remarry someone else by saying the Lord was leading them to do so. The response is simple: look to the code. The voice of God will never disagree with the revealed word of God. The Holy Spirit would never violate the Word of God inspired by the same Holy Spirit. That person is deceived and should be warned as heartily as Hermione warned Harry not to follow his vision of Sirius being tortured to go to the Department of Mysteries (see chapter one or *Harry Potter and the Order of the Phoenix*).

Some situations are not covered in Scripture, although we may feel an inclination toward one direction over another. We can ask ourselves whether such a decision would lead us closer to or further from God's overall calling on our life, and we can consider general guidelines the Bible gives that would apply to such situations. If it does not violate or lead away from anything in God's revealed moral will, and if it does not trouble our conscience, we are free to follow our inclination. If God doesn't want you going a certain way, he can make circumstances forbid it. All the while, however, we are free to operate as we choose. We should seek to be led by and obedient to our spiritual mentor, the Holy Spirit. We should also check with godly earthly mentors for confirmation of what we believe the Holy Spirit is leading us to do.

As we proceed to seek that which is good and fight evil, we must also align ourselves with allies on the side of good and eschew enemies who aim to harm us. We will take that up in the next chapter.

5

Sorting Out Allies from Enemies

> "'Don't you remember?' . . . 'About You-Know-Who.'
> He [Dumbledore] said, 'His gift for spreading discord
> and enmity is very great. We can fight it only by
> showing an equally strong bond of friendship and
> trust.'"
>
> *Hermione to Ron and Harry,*
> *Harry Potter and the Order of the Phoenix*

As soon as our characters enter into their adventure they must bond with their allies and beware their enemies. But it's a bit more complicated than that; most fantastic fiction includes the mythic archetype of the "shapeshifter"—someone who is not what they seem. So the good side must be analytical in choosing their teammates. We'll look at the shapeshifters later, for now we will focus on identifiable allies and enemies.

When Edmund first meets the "queen" in *The Lion, the Witch and the Wardrobe,* he has to decide whether she is friend or foe. Immediately upon meeting Mr. and Mrs. Beaver, the children have to determine whether they can be trusted, whether the White Witch is a witch or the rightful queen of Narnia. When all the Pevensie children meet Narnian creatures and talking beasts, they have to determine who is on Aslan's side and who is on the side of evil. The consequences of these decisions are lasting—especially for Edmund, who initially made the wrong call. In *The Last Battle* we see a final dividing of characters throughout all seven stories: whether they have been allies or enemies of Aslan determines where they go in their afterlife.

In *Harry Potter and the Sorcerer's Stone,* Harry hasn't even arrived at Hogwarts before he meets Draco Malfoy at Madam Malkan's shop. There he hears about the sorting to be done on their arrival. Draco tells him about the "wrong sort" of wizards and offers to help him find the right sort. Harry wisely says he can find the right sort on his own. When Harry is being sorted he knows that those who have gone to the dark side all went into Slytherin; therefore he wishes, "Not Slytherin!" which prompts the Sorting Hat to put him in Gryffindor.

Early on Harry chooses allies on the good side. In *Harry Potter and the Goblet of Fire* Dumbledore calls for a parting of the ways to sort those against Voldemort from those who are not. Recognizing one's allies and enemies is a vital task in every fantastic story for being able to fight evil effectively.

It's not the level of skill or talent that marks someone as an ally to the hero team, but primarily their stand on the side of good and against evil. Even unlikely characters contribute to the team. In *Star Wars: A New Hope,* Luke begins with youthful inexperience, Princess Leia shows sophisticated dedication, Han Solo shows daring recklessness; but all come together to defeat the Empire. The Ewoks—small and unfamiliar with advanced technology—are highly unlikely warriors in *Star Wars: Return of the Jedi.* At first glance, the hero team could be excused for not recognizing their value. Luke and friends made the right choice in teaming up with them, however; their skills, courage and ingenuity help the hero team take down the technologically advanced forces of the Empire.

Likewise, in *The Lion, the Witch and the Wardrobe* each of the allies is given jobs to do; boys are assigned to battle positions while the girls are not intended to fight (the books reflect the prevailing view of the 1950s, when they were written: "Battles are ugly when women fight"). Susan and Lucy, with their particular gifts, are as much a part of the hero team as the boys. In *Prince Caspian* Peter, Edmund, Susan and Lucy are called back into Narnia by Susan's horn because their help is desperately needed by allies of Prince Caspian, but Trumpkin is disappointed at first sight of them. He expects great warriors, not children. They have to demonstrate their skills to convince him they could be formidable allies. Reepicheep the mouse volunteers the services of the "gnawers and nibblers" whose unexpected help once freed Aslan from his bonds on the Stone Table.

In *Harry Potter and the Order of the Phoenix,* the formation of Dumbledore's Army comes about with such unlikely heroes as Neville Longbottom and Luna Lovegood, who prove essential to defeating the Death Eaters. There are even some unsavory characters, like Mundungus Fletcher, tolerated among the allies because of the valuable role they could play for the Order of the Phoenix; although Molly Weasley did her best to curb Fletcher's misbehavior and limit his unsavory influence on others.

ALLIES AS A UNIT

A group of allies is essential; even the Lone Ranger depended on Tonto. As allies learn to get along for the sake of a cause, readers learn much about friendship, commitment, loyalty and trust. We learn how various abilities work together for the common good, how to appreciate differences, how to resolve conflict and how to love. Princess Leia has to depend on the daring recklessness of Han Solo and Luke Skywalker to free her when Darth Vader holds her captive in *Star Wars: A New Hope.* Luke and Han need her political savvy, connections and devotion, watching her and learning from her as they progressed. The man, Han Solo, who was made a general gained some of his civility through the influence of Princess Leia.

We see a tight bond between Harry and Ron in *Harry Potter and the*

Sorcerer's Stone, before they even arrive at Hogwarts. Their alliance helps save Hermione from a mountain troll. And once they accept Hermione as an ally, her keen intelligence and knowledge help them get past all the enchantments protecting the Sorcerer's Stone (not to mention helping them with their studies). Ron pitches in with his bravery and expertise at chess to get them through the life-size chess game. This alliance ultimately helps Harry reach the Sorcerer's Stone to defeat Professor Quirrell and Voldemort. In each book, their alliance remains vital to the defeat of evil.

No matter who you are, there are times in life's journey that require the help of others. Everyone needs a hero team, a few trustworthy friends for whom you will sacrifice and who will make sacrifices for you to help you in your quest. Harry Potter's hero team includes Remus Lupin, Sirius Black, Professor McGonagall, the Weasleys and others in the Order of the Phoenix. They had been in the Order with Harry's parents and now stand together to help Harry. Lupin teaches Harry the Patronus Charm to ward off Dementors and shows him how to defeat a Boggart. Sirius fulfills his role as godfather. Mrs. Weasley takes on the motherly role vacated when Lily Potter died. All of these, beside his fellow Gryffindors and members of the Defense Association, make up the hero team that helps Harry in his quests.

BEWARE YOUR ENEMIES

Once the hero is established and alliances formed, the hero team must identify their enemies—those aligned with evil or refusing to ally themselves with good. The hero team must beware of their enemies and counter their schemes. Without this kind of understanding they would not be able to oppose them. Therefore, the allies must figure out who can be trusted and who can't.

This process of identifying enemies usually comes up early in the story. Luke realizes the Sand People are enemies, since they try to kill him as soon as he gets near enough. But enemies are not always so easy to identify. In *The Lion, the Witch and the Wardrobe* Lucy accepts Mr. Tumnus as an ally because he acts friendly. She does not realize he is in the pay of the White Witch. When Edmund arrives in Narnia he meets the witch, who introduces herself to him as Queen of Narnia. Similarly, Harry Potter has to choose whether Draco Malfoy will be his friend or enemy. Seeing that Malfoy hates anyone with less than pure wizard blood, despises the poor and displays arrogance, Harry declines his offer of friendship and makes him an enemy.

Scripture warns us that "bad company corrupts good morals," and that we are to be careful of our companions. Psalm 1 declares it not good to "sit in the seat of scoffers" or "stand in the way of sinners." We need to be careful who we allow into our lives in a close and personal way. This not only applies to people openly devoted to an ungodly lifestyle but sometimes Christians who are acting as enemies or who have given their lives over to something wrong. In life, unfortunately, sometimes we will encounter enemies within our Christian family who have set themselves against us. We need to face this and deal with it.

We are commanded to love our enemies and to pray for those who despitefully use us, but we are not told to make ourselves vulnerable to them. In 2 Timothy 4:14-15 Paul warns Timothy about an enemy: "Alexander the metal worker did me a great deal of harm." Paul doesn't take vengeance on Alexander, however; he left room for God to pass judgment: "The Lord will repay him for what he has done." Nevertheless, Paul warns Timothy to "be on your guard against him, because he strongly opposed our message." Identifying and guarding against enemies without resorting to doing evil against them: this is the wise approach.

HOPE FOR CHANGE

Even though those aligned with Voldemort in the Harry Potter series are rightly considered enemies, Dumbledore allows people to shift allegiances. Here's a good example of how difficult it can be to sort out allies from enemies, especially when one may be concealing his true loyalties. Severus Snape bears the Dark Mark and was once a Death Eater, but he is allowed to join the Order of the Phoenix. So is Snape a repentant enemy turned ally or a true enemy who has tricked Dumbledore into believing him?

There are times when discretion and covert activity is necessary to deal with those who are working on the side of evil, as when Rahab was rewarded for hiding the Hebrew spies and misleading the men of Jericho about the Hebrew spies' whereabouts. We should expect deception to be at work on the side of evil, or even to test devotion to good, and therefore give up our gullibility. In 1 Kings 13 there is a strange story of a "man of God" being deceived by an "old prophet," a prophet who convinced him that God had sent an angel to tell this man of God to dine with the old prophet. This was direct disobedience to God's command that the man of God was not to eat or drink in that place. As a result the "man of God" was attacked by a lion and killed. The man of God was deceived, tested by one who seemed to be on the hero team. He should have been more careful. Similarly, at the parting of the ways some covert activity becomes crucial to protect the wizarding world from Voldemort and his followers. "Constant vigilance!" the imposter of Mad-Eye Moody repeatedly teaches. Jesus put it another way: "I am sending you out like sheep among wolves. Therefore be as shrewd as snakes and as innocent as doves" (Matthew 10:16).

Sorting out allies from enemies is not about finding out who is on *our* side; it's about finding out who is on the side of good. Dumbledore understood this clearly when he told Cornelius Fudge that Voldemort had returned. "The only one against whom I intend to work," said Dumbledore, "is Lord Voldemort. If you are against him, then we remain, Cornelius, on the same side."

We see a similar situation in the Bible when Joshua crosses into the Promised Land for the first time and approaches Jericho.

> He looked up and saw a man standing in front of him with a drawn sword in his hand. Joshua went up to him and asked, "Are you for us or for our enemies?"
>
> "Neither," he replied, "but as commander of the army of the LORD I have now come." (Joshua 5:13-14)

The question is not about who is on our side, but whether we are on God's side. As we approach life's battles, we must ask ourselves how we can take our place on God's side, fighting against evil.

ALLIES MUST STAND UNITED!

In fantasy stories, as in life, one of the enemy's primary aims is to cause disunity and dissension among the allies on the good side. In *Star Wars: The Empire Strikes Back,* Darth Vader forces Lando Calrissian to betray Han Solo and Princess Leia at the Cloud City. In *The Lion, the Witch and the Wardrobe,* the White Witch separates Edmund from his siblings and seeks to turn him against them. In *Harry Potter and the Goblet of Fire*, Dumbledore tries to get Severus Snape and Sirius Black to lay aside old differences, but they refuse to let go of their mutual loathing. Dumbledore tells them, "You will shake hands. You are on the same side now. Time is short, and unless the few of us who know the truth stand united, there is no hope for any of us." This is good advice for all those on the side of good to remember, especially when issues divide us.

Even the most rugged heroes need allies. Even Han Solo—whose very name implies he'd prefer to go it alone—relies on his faithful first mate, Chewbacca the Wookiee, and eventually a few others. There is great benefit to having a close friend, committed to help you through life. The book of Ecclesiastes puts it this way:

Two are better than one,
    because they have a good return for their work.
If one falls down,
    his friend can help him up.
But pity the man who falls
    and has no one to help him up!
Also, if two lie down together, they will keep warm.
    But how can one keep warm alone?
Though one may be overpowered,
    two can defend themselves.
A cord of three strands is not quickly broken. (Ecclesiastes 4:9-12)

Beyond being a good "first mate," Chewbacca the Wookiee serves as an excellent example of a valuable ally. Generally Chewy is a good helper, putting up with Solo's erratic moods, showing affection, and faithfully copiloting the Millennium Falcon. Even though Han indicates that a Wookiee might tear your head off if you win against him at a game, Chewy shows real care and compassion. While on the snowy plains of Hoth in *The Empire Strikes Back,* Han Solo endangers himself by going out into the frozen wilderness in search of Luke. As dusk approaches and the time comes for the shield doors to close, Han Solo isn't back with Luke. Chewy cries as his friend is closed outside and in danger. Chewbacca is brave and daring in battle, using his size and strength but also his ingenuity. He and one of the Ewoks take over one of the Empire's mechanized walkers in *Return of the Jedi*, then use it to blast their way into a shield generator defending the second Death Star. Chewy volunteers to go with Lando Calrissian to rescue Han Solo from Jabba the Hutt. However, the best example I see of what to look for in a friend or ally for your hero team is seen when Chewbacca comes to the rescue of C-3PO.

C-3PO is torn to pieces and left in a junk pile on Cloud City in *The Empire Strikes Back*. Chewbacca goes looking for him, crying over his condition when he finds C-3PO dismantled. He retrieves the pieces and sets to work trying to put the droid back together. When C-3PO regains his head but still doesn't have his legs attached, Chewy puts him on his back and carries him until he could finish putting him back together totally.

When C-3PO is so torn up he can't stand on his own two feet, Chewy carries him through. That kind of devotion is invaluable among the allies on your hero team. There will be times when we are overtaken by our own sins or the sins others commit against us, when the cares of life may overwhelm us, or when our financial or material lack will require the generosity of others to meet our needs. When we fall to pieces or are torn up, emotionally or spiritually, we will need friends who are willing to dig us out of the "junk pile" of life, lift us up, and carry us along if need be until we can stand on our own again.

The apostle Paul gives us an admonition in Galatians 6:1: "If someone is caught in a sin, you who are spiritual should restore him gently." The word translated "restore" is a medical term that describes setting a broken leg. Consider how you would uphold someone who couldn't stand on a broken leg, set that which is broken, and then support him until the break is healed enough to stand on. This is similar to how allies of Jesus Christ should treat each other when we get broken by our sin or the sin of others. We can get torn up in life's battles; finding friends like these before one needs them is of great value.

Galatians 6:2 goes on to say that we are to bear one another's burdens. The Living Bible says, "Share each other's troubles and problems." This is an integral part of being an active member of God's "hero team." We see an example of this in Acts 2:43-47 where early believers and followers of Jesus shared everything they had, shared their meals with great joy and generosity, and sold their possessions to share the proceeds with those in need.

It is essential for Christians to assemble a team of allies who will stand with us in the cause of good and support us when we need it, and whom we will support when they need it. Jesus never sent his disciples out alone. He also admonished them strongly that they must love one another as he had loved them. Jesus knew that the enemy of our cause has a gift for spreading discord and enmity, and that, in the words of Dumbledore, "we can fight it only by showing an equally strong bond of friendship and trust." Therefore, let us sort out our allies from our enemies, develop strong bonds of friendship and trust within our "hero team," and be on guard against our enemies. In this way we will be prepared to do good and overcome evil.

The next chapter deals with how to prepare ourselves for the ordeals we must surely face in our battle against evil.

6

Preparing for the Ordeal in Our Battle Against Evil

"I'm a *what?*" gasped Harry.

"A wizard, o'course," said Hagrid . . . an' a thumpin' good'un, I'd say, once yeh've been trained up a bit."

Harry Potter and the Sorcerer's Stone

In most fantastic stories both good and evil inhabit the extraordinary realm. Sides are already drawn before the hero crosses the threshold. A battle may be impending or already underway. However, the hero and hero team typically have a time of preparation before the battle. This includes military preparation, whether with a sword for Peter and Edmund and archery practice for Susan in the Chronicles of Narnia, a wand for Harry Potter and his friends, or a light saber for Luke Skywalker in *Star Wars: A New Hope*. It also requires mental preparation: Luke must master the Force, Harry and friends must take wizarding classes at Hogwarts School along with practice in the Defense Association. There is always need for preparation in the fight against evil, and the time to prepare is before the battle.

PREPARATION IS IMPERATIVE!

At the creation of Narnia, Aslan warns that a great evil has already come into their new world. The befuddled beasts think he said *a neevil*; they wonder what that might be and eventually settle on Uncle Andrew. Their initial remedy was to plant this "neevil" head first in the ground; they think his hair are roots and his legs branches. C. S. Lewis depicts their naiveté as silly—just as silly as we humans sometimes are when we disregard the danger of unrestrained evil in our midst. The fact that the inhabitants of Narnia are ignorant about evil and how to defend against it is deadly serious. Jadis—the real evil that prowls their world—has a history. Her use of the Deplorable Word to destroy her own sister and their entire world of Charn demonstrated her evil nature. Aslan commands the Narnian creatures to prepare themselves to fight against evil when it spreads in their world, as he knows it will in time.

In *Harry Potter and the Goblet of Fire*, Minister of Magic Cornelius Fudge does not prepare to fight evil because he dares not see it for the threat it is. He tries to stay neutral, but this proves to be a huge mistake. His refusal to prepare leaves the wizarding world more vulnerable, and he is put out of his position. Those on the side of good must use the time between battles to prepare for the next one, or they might lose all they hold dear.

Scripture tells us we are not fighting against flesh and blood but against spiritual influences of evil that inspire the actors in our world's dramas. We need to be aware of any weaknesses that might leave us vulnerable and prepare ourselves to meet the dangers and temptations we might rightfully anticipate. Whether in the cosmic realm, world politics, or our personal or spiritual lives, we must expect a conflict between good and evil and prepare ourselves for the battles sure to come.

PREPARE THROUGH TRAINING

In the *Star Wars* movies, everyone who wants to become a Jedi must go through training, including military skills like using a light saber in combat and flying well. Jedis are also trained in patience, obedience and submission to the Jedi Council. Anakin Skywalker does well in military training, but his self-promotion, impatience and unwillingness to submit to the judgment of the Jedi Council leave him vulnerable to the dark side. Obi-Wan Kenobi gives Luke Skywalker his father's light saber and trains him in the Force and the Jedi Code, and Yoda trains Luke in concentration and self-control as he learns more about using the Force. Yoda sends Luke into a cave to face a manifestation of Darth Vader as further preparation for the battles—mental, military and spiritual—that await him.

In the Harry Potter series, schooling at Hogwarts School is meant to prepare students to take up a productive place in wizarding society and to fight against the Dark Arts. Students are tested on what they've read and learned in class, and they practice defensive spells. Harry and his friends know that preparation and practice are essential to prepare them for the inevitable showdown with Voldemort, so when a new administration refuses to prepare students to *really* fight evil, they meet in the Room of Requirement, which provides them with whatever they need to practice defense against the dark arts.

Unlikely Heroes: Everyone Must Prepare to Join the Fight

The battle between good and evil is all-inclusive. When it comes to fighting evil, everyone is needed in the battle and no one can escape it. There is no one too great or too lowly to contribute. In Narnia, Reepicheep and the other mice are among the most valiant warriors in the battle against the White Witch. When Susan and Lucy are unable to untie the cords which bind Aslan's dead body, the mice nibble away at the ropes, playing a role they were uniquely gifted to perform. Aslan is resurrected and forever remembers their contribution. Small does not mean useless if those small ones have prepared themselves to work on the side of good as only they can.

In *Harry Potter and the Order of the Phoenix*, Neville Longbottom, Ginny Weasley and Luna Lovegood hardly seemed powerful enough to survive against the Death Eaters, much less win! At one point Harry wants to leave them behind while he, Ron, and Hermione go to the Ministry of Magic to rescue Sirius, but they will not be put off. They have trained to fight evil in the Defense Association, and they take that seriously. Each one does their part in the battle. Luna's connections to the press prove useful in getting the truth out to the public when Harry needs the power of truth. These unlikely heroes become powerful opponents to the Death Eaters and Voldemort not because of inherent greatness but because they were prepared and determined.

The Millennium Falcon isn't the biggest, or best ship we encounter in the *Star Wars* series, but when Han Solo wholeheartedly devotes it to serve the Alliance, it does the job. Even Luke Skywalker hardly seems a match for the Dark Side—even Yoda doubts him when he first begins his training—but it turns out that Luke can be trained.

So can everyone in God's kingdom. I can say this, because it is not our size, strength or technical ability that makes us mighty in God's kingdom, it is the power of God at work through us. What does our preparation look like in terms of personal and spiritual development? We gain some insight from the first chapter of 2 Peter: "Grace and peace be multiplied to you in the knowledge of God and of Jesus our Lord" (2 Peter 1:2 NASB). Anyone willing to learn the *knowledge* of God and of Jesus our Lord, available in the Bible, can experience God's grace and peace.

Where do we get what we need? What is in our metaphorical "Room of Requirement"? Peter says, "*His divine power* has given us everything we need for life and godliness." This is God's gift, not our natural resources. "Through our *knowledge of him who has called us* by his own glory and goodness" (2 Peter 1:3). Those willing to be trained in the knowledge of

God can be, but there's more to it than training: "He has given us his *very great and precious promises*, so that *through them* you may *participate in the divine nature* and escape the corruption in the world caused by evil desires" (2 Peter 1:4).

It's not book knowledge that will defeat evil even on our best day! It's becoming partakers of God's nature though knowledge of him and employment of his "very great and precious promises" that empower us to overcome corruption and evil.

Here's a quick illustration of how to use God's promises to battle against evil desires. It's so simple a child can learn to practice it. God's word promises that, "The one who is in you"—God, the indwelling Christ, the Holy Spirit—"is greater than the one who is in the world"— the evil one. So when we are faced with an alluring temptation, we can claim that promise and pray for God's divine nature to operate on our behalf.

We know it is God's will for us to overcome temptation and not act on evil desires, therefore, we can trust in another of God's promises:

> This is the confidence we have in approaching God: that if we ask anything according to his will, he hears us. And if we know that he hears us—whatever we ask—we know that we have what we asked of him. (1 John 5:14-15)

So by knowing, believing and invoking these two promises, we have a way to approach God for his help so that we can escape the corruption that is in our world.

Peter goes on to give us a study list for a lifetime of progressive training:

- add to your faith goodness
- and to goodness, knowledge
- and to knowledge, self-control
- and to self-control, perseverance

- and to perseverance, godliness
- and to godliness, brotherly kindness
- and to brotherly kindness, love

This progression is one that any disciple can follow, with this promise:

> For if you possess these qualities in increasing measure, they will keep you from being ineffective and unproductive in your knowledge of our Lord Jesus Christ. (2 Peter 1:5-8)

We are meant to be effective and productive; our knowledge is meant to empower and prepare us for useful service on God's hero team. This requires considerable dedication and effort to gain the knowledge that can empower and prepare us for the battles we will face.

Of course, no one can win such battles alone. All members of the hero team—even the most unlikely—are needed in the fight against evil. Therefore, we need to prepare together and figure out where our gifts and abilities fit when working as part of a team. Each individual contributes particular strengths, knowledge, skills and abilities which work together to thwart evil. We see this kind of cooperation in our fantasy stories. In the Harry Potter series, for example, kids are aligned by their houses, by school and by their loyalty to Dumbledore or to Voldemort. Similarly, we must align ourselves with others committed to Jesus Christ and the kingdom of God, with others in our local community who are working for good causes, with a particular church family under the leadership of gifted leaders, and with a small group of committed friends who make up our hero team, and on whose hero team we serve. We are more powerful as we unify. Finding and cementing our place in such a network is an important part of our preparation.

Fantastic stories allow us to contemplate the ideas behind battles between good and evil. They also raise the question of whether evil is an entity or something else. The battle against evil is personal. Therefore, by knowing the nature of the "evil one" we can better anticipate, prepare for and avoid the kind of schemes he would come up with. So part of our preparation is to get to know the nature of the villain, which we will look at thoroughly in another chapter. We should also be aware of our unique nature and areas of weakness because the enemy will seek to exploit us at our weak points.

Hermione has the right idea when she warns Harry at the end of *Harry Potter and the Order of the Phoenix* that Voldemort knows his nature. Harry should beware of being lured into the Ministry of Magic by him. Hermione knows the nature of the evil one and that Voldemort could take advantage of Harry's nature. How differently might that school year have ended if Harry had been as aware of Voldemort as Voldemort was aware of Harry?

PREPARING TO USE SUPERNATURAL GIFTS TO FIGHT EVIL

The mentor usually gives the hero or hero team gifts to help in their quest. Obi-Wan Kenobi gives Luke Skywalker his father's light saber. Headmaster Dumbledore gives Harry Potter his father's invisibility cloak. Sirius Black gives Harry a Firebolt broomstick, which later helps him get past a dragon in the Triwizard Tournament. In *The Lion, the Witch and the Wardrobe,* Father Christmas (a wise old man if ever there was one) brings gifts—not the toys we associate with Santa Claus but tools to be used in battle:

- to Peter, a sword and shield with the Lion emblazoned on it
- to Susan, a magic horn which will bring help if blown in times of extreme need, and a bow and arrows which will not easily miss
- to Lucy, a small bottle made of diamond holding an elixir made from the fire flowers of the sun, which will heal those who are wounded

Each of these gifts in our various stories requires some practice or preparation to use them. Likewise, God gives us gifts which we are supposed to prepare ourselves to use. The apostle Paul tells Timothy not to neglect the gift that is in him (1 Timothy 4:4) and again to "stir up" his gift (2 Timothy 1:6). The gifts are given freely, but they come with the responsibility to use them well by honing our skills, and acquainting ourselves with where they might be of most service. The Bible speaks of spiritual gifts in 1 Corinthians 12—14, ministerial gifts in Ephesians 4 and gifts specific to individuals in Romans 12 (studying any of these chapters would be an excellent form of preparation to use our gifts well).

Whatever our gifts, they are not given to us *for* us; they are given *to* us for the good of the whole hero team.

> There are different kinds of gifts, but the same Spirit. There are different kinds of service, but the same Lord. There are different kinds of working, but the same God works all of them in all men. Now to each one the manifestation of the Spirit is given *for the common good*. (1 Corinthians 12:4-7)

The readiness of the hero team depends on individuals faithfully exercising their gifts. The whole body of Christ cannot be fully prepared without each individual part of that body exercising the gifts each one has been given to benefit others. We need to learn about these gifts, identify which gifts we have, and practice using them because in our world and our spiritual lives—as in Narnia—our gifts are tools not toys.

PRACTICE WITH GOD'S ARMOR AND WEAPONS

The Bible speaks of our battle against evil in military terms. What good soldier goes into battle without having practiced putting on his protective gear and using his weapons? None! One of the things I like best about the Chronicles of Narnia is that children master the use of weapons in the battle against evil. Even a child can learn to use God's armor and spiritual weapons—both defensive and offensive—because God will help anyone seeking to serve him. In our spiritual adventure, we prepare by learning to "put on the full armor of God" and practice using the spiritual weapons of salvation, righteousness, faith, truth, prayer, God's word and a readiness to share the gospel.

We don't prepare just by reading about our spiritual weapons and armor, any more that just reading Professor Umbrage's *Defense Against the Dark Arts* text would prepare Harry Potter to defeat evil; we have to *practice* and *learn* to use them well. The biblical instructions for such preparation (quoted below from Ephesians 6:10-18) are quite detailed:

- *"Be strong in the Lord and in his mighty power."* We must practice reminding ourselves that it is not by our might or by our power, but by the power of God in us that great feats will be accomplished.

- *"Put on the full armor of God so that you can take your stand against the devil's schemes."* Part of our preparation is indoctrination; we must realize who and what we are fighting against.

- *"Our struggle is not against flesh and blood, but against the rulers, against the authorities, against the powers of this dark world and against the spiritual forces of evil in the heavenly realms."* We must study the Bible to understand what it reveals about the spiritual forces arrayed against us.

- *"Put on the full armor of God, so that when the day of evil comes, you may be able to stand your ground, and after you have done everything, to stand."* Notice this says *"when* the day of evil comes"—not *if*. Every one on God's hero team will see a day when they must confront evil, so preparation is essential.

Use the following self-examination to see how well prepared you are in the use of your spiritual armor and weapons. Ephesians calls on us to "stand firm" with

- *The belt of truth buckled around your waist.* What is true? How do you distinguish truth from deception? Is your life true or are you hiding things, deceiving anyone? How do you know your beliefs are true?

How do you know the Bible is true? How do you know what you are being taught is true? Truth holds our protective gear together; what can you do to tighten your "belt of truth"? Do it!

- *The breastplate of righteousness.* Do you rely on being good enough to please God? What will protect your heart when the enemy attacks, accusing you of sin and telling you that you will never be good enough to please God? According to Philippians 3:9, it is Christ's righteousness that covers us.

- *Your feet fitted with the readiness that comes from the gospel of peace.* Do you have your marching boots on? Are you ready to go out to share the good news of God's love with others? Can you give a reason for the hope within you? Do you know God's story well enough to pass it on to others? Can you answer basic questions about your faith?

- *The shield of faith, with which you can extinguish all the flaming arrows of the evil one.* Are you ready to repel those "fiery darts" the enemy assails us with? He will try to set us on fire with lust, envy, greed, hatred, doubt. He will try to burn down our happy homes. Faith will shield us. How are you building your faith? Faith comes by asking questions like Thomas asked to rid ourselves of our doubts, by hearing the Word of God. Are you asking questions so that your faith can be upheld? How strong is the arm that holds up your shield of faith? Are there others who hold the same kind of faith as yours who can lift up their faith shields alongside yours to create a wall of safety?

- *The helmet of salvation.* How do you *know* you are saved? On what basis dare you say that you know you have eternal life? How can you claim your sins have been forgiven? Do you know God's Word well enough that you will not be shaken if the enemy tries to make you worry about your salvation? Ask someone on your church staff or a Christian you trust to help you gain or maintain assurance of your salvation.

- *The sword of the Spirit, which is the word of God.* Have you examined the Bible thoroughly? Have you neglected it lately? Are you handling the word of God accurately? Are you practiced enough in God's Word that you will be strong enough for a prolonged battle?

How well would you do if you were examined on your knowledge and use of God's armor and weaponry? Students at Hogwarts are examined in their O.W.L. or N.E.W.T. tests, but it's not just the grade on paper that really matters. As the Defense Association understands, what matters is how well prepared they are to *use* what they learn in defense against the dark arts. When confronted with evil, set to destroy them, they need to know their stuff but also be practiced enough to use their knowledge well. So too with us, our participation in and preparation to use the protective gear and weapons God gives is essential to the outcome of the battles we will face.

So practice! Paul finishes with this admonition: "And pray in the Spirit on all occasions with all kinds of prayers and requests. With this in mind, be alert and always keep on praying for all the saints" (Ephesians 6:18). Once our armor is in place, weapons in hand, we are to *always keep on* praying. When Harry Potter is fighting against Tom Riddle and the Basilisk in the Chamber of Secrets, he recalls that Dumbledore promised he would always be there for any who remained loyal to him, and that help would be given to all who asked. So in the heat of battle, with the King of Snakes coming for him, Harry cries out for help. It comes in the form of the sword of Godric Gryffindor, the Phoenix and the Sorting Hat. Jesus taught his disciples to pray, "Lead us not into temptation, but deliver us from evil," or "the evil one." We would do well to remember in the heat of our battles to cry out in prayer for help greater than ourselves.

We will face the battle against evil on a mundane level (like defending against bullies on the playground), a spiritual level (in our inner battle against sin) and worldwide on a political level. So our preparation needs to be applicable in all areas of life. And it is crucial that we take our preparation seriously, being sober and alert. We must not take unnecessary chances with our physical lives, our relationships and our spiritual purity. We must prepare for the battles to come and never let our guard down. There will always be tests, trials, difficulties and suffering in this world, but we are to be of good cheer because Jesus has overcome the world. However, we are also to dedicate ourselves to be prepared to do our very best in the battle against evil. This is a serious endeavor and preparation can make all the difference when the battles arrive.

7

Tests, Trials, Tricksters and Threshold Guardians

"I have told you these things, so that in me you may have peace. In this world you will have trouble."

Jesus, to his disciples (John 16:33)

No sooner do heroes enter the extraordinary world than a series of tests, challenges and trials confronts them. These allow a hero to learn, gain strength, exercise courage and develop skills that will be needed further along in the journey.

The 2005 movie *Batman Begins* offers an illustration of a hero recognizing the proper function of tests and trials. Bruce Wayne (Batman-to-be) is confronted in prison by a menacing fellow prisoner. This brute of a man assaults Bruce Wayne, and growls, "I am the devil!" Bruce Wayne replies, "You're not the devil; you're practice." He then proceeds to fight back and conquer his oversized opponent.

When characters face tests, trials and challenges, they will have the normal fears and temptations, but this too is practice. They may make mistakes and wrong choices, and will have to deal with the consequences of their lapses or successes. The heroes will also have to deal with tricksters and threshold guardians who bar the way to their intended goal.

TESTS, TRIALS AND CHALLENGES

Luke Skywalker is tested repeatedly in the *Star Wars* series. He must fend off sand people, fly dangerous missions, strike at the Death Star and extricate himself from bonds while hanging upside-down in the cave of a snow monster lest he be eaten. He must find a way into Jabba the Hutt's palace to rescue Han Solo, Leia, C-3PO and R2-D2. He must get himself and his friends out of danger after being sentenced to be terminated by the dread Sarlac, in whose belly—C-3PO translates for Jabba—"you will find a new definition of pain and suffering as you are digested over a thousand years." He must battle Darth Vader and resist temptation to turn to the dark side. He must pass inner tests of patience and resistance against hatred and anger. In these and other ways he must prove himself.

Each book in the Harry Potter series covers a year in his life and has challenges that must be met. It's difficult enough, we learn in *Harry Potter and the Sorcerer's Stone,* for Harry to grow up an orphan, living with relatives like the Dursleys. Then in his first year he has to help capture a mountain troll, get past a three-headed dog named Fluffy, escape Devil's Snare, find and catch the correct flying key among a flock, win a game of living chess, figure out which potion is safe to drink, and finally face Professor Quirrell/Voldemort and get the Sorcerer's Stone out of the Mirror of Erised.

In Harry's second year he has to discover who the heir of Slytherin is and defeat the monster in the Chamber of Secrets. In his third year he and Hermione are called on to figure out how to rescue Buckbeak and Sirius. In his fourth year Harry has to get through the Triwizard Tournament, which involves taking a golden egg from the nest of a mother dragon, rescuing hostages held by merpeople, and getting through a dangerous maze to reach the Triwizard Cup. Then he has to overcome

Voldemort and the Death Eaters. In Harry's fifth year he is in danger of being expelled and having his wand confiscated. He is tested in every subject for his Ordinary Wizarding Level examinations (O.W.L.s). Later he and members of the Defense Association have to figure out how to get transportation from Hogwarts to London, where they battle Death Eaters and Voldemort. In his sixth year, Harry goes with Dumbledore to find and destroy one of Voldemort's horcruxes. Together they face terrible challenges, including a lake guarded by inferius (animated human corpses). All such tests and trials prepare the hero team to confront evil more effectively as the story progresses.

Tests, trials and challenges may seem terrible and frightening as they are happening; however, they are a necessary part of the hero's training and preparation of the hero team to ultimately defeat evil. The Bible describes the purpose of the believer's tests, trials, and challenges in a similarly useful way. Some expect that being on God's side means life gets easier. While that may be the picture some evangelists paint to attract people, anyone who begins to read the Bible may be surprised at the severe tests, trials, challenges and difficulties faced by those on God's side. The apostle Peter made this clear in his letter to suffering Christians:

> Dear friends, do not be surprised at the painful trial you are suffering, as though something strange were happening to you. But rejoice that you participate in the suffering of Christ, so that you may be overjoyed when his glory is revealed. (1 Peter 4:12-13)

The apostle James points out the benefits of going through trials:

> Consider it pure joy, my brothers, whenever you face trials of many kinds, because you know that the testing of your faith develops perseverance. Perseverance must finish its work so that you may be mature and complete, not lacking anything. (James 1:2-4)

Peter emphasizes the necessity of trials for those on God's side:

These have come so that your faith—of greater worth than gold, which perishes even though refined by fire—may be proved genuine and may result in praise, glory and honor when Jesus Christ is revealed. (1 Peter 1:6-7)

Herein we see a purpose to tests, trials and challenges. When we see a hero team face difficulties and trials, we may feel tension but trust that the author is not going to let permanent damage come to the good side. Even death is shown to be an enemy that can be faced and overcome. Even when beloved characters die, there remains a sense that their death must serve some greater good. There may even remain a sense of hope and expectation that death is not the end for those on the side of good.

Likewise, when we face trials, obstacles, tests, temptations, fears and challenges of every kind in our lives, we can have hope and confidence that the Author of our story is allowing us to be tested to develop good character qualities and the strong faith we will need to fulfill our purpose in his story. We can even face death assured that God's kingdom goes on after death, where all our tests and trials will pay off in glory.

FACING FEARS AND TEMPTATIONS

A hero team has to face trials, tests and challenges, but they also must face their fears. When Luke Skywalker tries to convince Yoda to take him on as an apprentice, he says, "I am not afraid!"

To this Yoda sagely replies, "Yeah, you will be. You will be." A key part of facing tests and trials is learning to face one's fears.

In *Harry Potter and the Chamber of Secrets*, students practice facing their fears in class with the help of Boggarts—shape-shifters that take on the form of one's greatest fear. Ron, who is terrified of spiders, faces a Boggart that turns into an eight-foot tall spider. Ron learns to use the *Riddiculus* spell, and the spider's legs disappear leaving it spinning on the floor. This classroom exercise is preparation for a time when Ron will

have to brave a nest of enormous talking, man-eating spiders while seeking to stop a monster that has been released from the Chamber of Secrets. Harry's greatest fear is Dementors, horrible creatures that suck all
hope and happiness out of everyone near them, leaving the person with
only their most horrible memory. When he is near a Dementor, Harry
hears his father and mother's screams as they were being murdered. Professor Lupin helps Harry practice facing that fear by learning to conjure
a patronus to drive away Dementors. Harry uses this knowledge and
confidence born of practice to save Sirius, Dudley and himself from Dementors poised to suck out their souls.

A hero team also has to face temptations in the course of their journey,
as do we all. The temptations in Narnia are considerable. In *The Magician's Nephew* Digory has to decide whether to believe and obey Aslan by
bringing him the fruit of the Tree of Protection without tasting it. He is
tempted to sneak a taste, as the White Witch did. The White Witch also
tempts him with altruistic longings when she suggests that he could save
his mother's life if he would take the fruit and use the rings to return to
his world. Digory resists that temptation; consequently his mother is
eventually healed. In *The Lion, the Witch and the Wardrobe* Edmund is en-
snared by a temptation provided by the White Witch in an enchanted
form of his favorite food, Turkish Delight, and in promises of luxury and
glory. In *Prince Caspian,* prodded along by Nikabrik the dwarf when
things are not going their way in the battle, some on Caspian's side are
tempted to find power by calling up the White Witch. They do not realize that help from the great kings and queens of Narnia is already at the
door. This time of temptation is also a test that reveals who is truly on
Aslan's side and who is on the side of evil and must be destroyed.

In *Star Wars: Revenge of the Sith,* Anakin Skywalker is tempted to turn
to the dark side by promises that he could save Padmé (whom he
dreamed would die in childbirth). He falls for the Emperor's temptation,
does not pass the test and loses his battle against Obi-Wan Kenobi. His

mutilated remains are turned into Darth Vader. His defection to the dark side devastates Padmé so much that she loses her will to live. Instead of saving her by giving in to the Emperor, Anakin's defection to the dark side leads to her death shortly after giving birth to Luke and Leia. This leaves Darth Vader alone, guilty, and trapped in his evil shell. All of this proceeded from Anakin yielding to temptation.

In *Harry Potter and the Sorcerer's Stone,* Hagrid is tempted with a dragon's egg. He has always wanted to raise a dragon, and the evil one knows his secret illicit desires. So Quirrell, disguised as a stranger at the Hog's Head, lets Hagrid win a dragon's egg, all the while plying him with drinks and extracting information needed to get past the guard dog, Fluffy, to the Sorcerer's Stone. When Hagrid gives into that temptation, even though he knows it is illegal, he puts many in jeopardy. The information he surrenders gives the evil one access to the Sorcerer's Stone, along with the wealth and long life it promised. Later Hagrid shows sincere remorse, but only after realizing the danger and harm he has caused. The reader can learn things from Hagrid's experience that reflect the Bible teaching about the nature of temptation. James writes,

> When tempted, no one should say, "God is tempting me." For God cannot be tempted by evil, nor does he tempt anyone; but each one is tempted when, by his own evil desire, he is dragged away and enticed. Then, after desire has conceived, it gives birth to sin; and sin, when it is full-grown, gives birth to death. (James 1:13-15)

Look at this progression with Hagrid as our example. Hagrid is enticed by his own desire for an illegal dragon's egg. The dragon's egg, tended lovingly in Hagrid's fireplace, gives birth to baby Norbert. Norbert grows, and predictably the danger of death grows with him—which we see when Norbert bites Ron. Hermione points out the inevitable danger: Hagrid is neglecting important parts of his life to hide the illegal dragon; dragons breathe fire; and Hagrid lives in a wooden hut!

Anyone who wasn't emotionally invested in protecting his secret passion would have seen that this was not going to lead anywhere good. It was clear to everyone but Hagrid that his temptation had turned to sin—although no one called it that—and unrestrained sin is bound to grow and with that growth bring increasing danger. Hagrid is so caught up in protecting his secret illegal passion that he is not reasonable. He loves his little sin and guards it to make sure no one takes it away from him. He neglects his duties, becomes secretive and puts his position at Hogwarts, his friendships and the people he cares about most at risk.

How have you prepared yourself to deal with temptation in areas where you know you are weak or vulnerable? Are you keenly aware of any illicit desires you nurse along, hiding them so that no one will interfere? Have you surrounded yourself with good friends with whom you can share your secrets and pray about your temptations before they hatch? Are you willing to allow them to help you get rid of illicit and dangerous things that may be growing under your care? Even the most disciplined among us are prone to temptation and must prepare *in advance* to step away from it before it becomes big enough to devour us and the good in our lives. The Bible promises,

> No temptation has seized you except what is common to man. And God is faithful; he will not let you be tempted beyond what you can bear. But when you are tempted he will also provide a way out so that you can stand up under it. (1 Corinthians 10:13)

This is one of those promises that we should memorize, believe, depend on and think about deeply. By reflection on God's word and through experience, I've concluded that the "way out" is like an exit on a freeway: it usually comes up earlier than you expect. We must flee temptation *before* we get so far down the road that we've passed the exit God provides. As Yoda lay dying in *Return of the Jedi*, he warns Luke, "Once you start down the dark path, forever will it dominate your destiny." We should seriously heed such a warning. Exit the road of temptation before you start down any dark path.

TRICKSTERS

Everybody needs a few laughs, right? The mythic archetype of the trickster brings mischief, distraction and sometimes the opportunity for change. Peeves the Poltergeist is a classic mischief-making trickster in the Harry Potter series. He is continually disruptive, but he manages to help Harry out by distracting Filch when Harry is about to get in trouble. Tricksters are often comic sidekicks, a role played nicely by George and Fred Weasley who provide a few laughs when things get tense for Harry Potter. At the end of the *Goblet of Fire*, Harry gives Fred and George his winnings to start their joke shop. "If you don't take it," he tells them, "I'm throwing it down the drain. I don't want it and I don't need it. But I could do with a few laughs. We could all do with a few laughs. I've got a feeling we're going to need them more than usual before long."

The trickster can create impish accidents or slips of the tongue that alert us to the need for change. In Luke's first encounter with Yoda in *The Empire Strikes Back,* his soon-to-be mentor plays the role of a trickster to show Luke that he needs to change.

One might be hard-pressed to think of a classic trickster in the Bible, but Balaam's donkey (Numbers 22) certainly has a slip of the tongue. The donkey spoke in Balaam's native language to alert him and the reader to the need for immediate change. The donkey could see the angel of the Lord standing in his path, holding a drawn sword, but Balaam—blinded by his greed—could not. If the donkey had not started talking, Balaam would have been struck down.

THRESHOLD GUARDIANS

Threshold guardians function as gatekeepers along a hero's path. The sand people in *Star Wars: A New Hope* are threshold guardians, keeping

Luke initially from finding Obi-Wan Kenobi. Fluffy, the three-headed dog guarding a trapdoor in *Harry Potter and the Sorcerer's Stone* is reminiscent of another mythical threshold guardian, Cerberus, the three headed dog who guards the way to the underworld in Greek mythology. The merpeople and grindylows were threshold guardians in the underwater task of the Triwizard Tournament of *Harry Potter and the Goblet of Fire,* to make sure the rules were followed. The dragons, Sphinx, blast-ended-skrewts and other obstacles in the maze were likewise threshold guardians. So are the Whomping Willow and the portrait of the Fat Lady that guards the entrance to the Gryffindor common room; a threshold guardian is not necessarily an enemy but one who guards entrances.

There are various ways a hero can get by a threshold guardian: outwit it, use a password, appease it (Fluffy is appeased by music), befriend it, solve a puzzle (as with the Sphinx) or, metaphorically speaking, get into its skin. One way to get past threshold guardians is to become one with those standing in the way. Luke and Han Solo don the uniforms of Imperial storm troopers in *Star Wars: A New Hope* to rescue Princess Leia from the prison cell block of the Death Star. Harry and Ron use polyjuice potion and became Crabbe and Goyle to get into the Slytherin common room in the *Chamber of Secrets.* Chewbacca and an Ewok get into the Empire's mechanized walker on Endor as a ruse to access the shield protecting the second Death Star in *Return of the Jedi.*

A threshold guardian may be a character, a locked door, secret vault, a force of nature, an animal (like the wolf guarding the gate to the White Witch's castle in *The Lion, the Witch and the Wardrobe*), guards, sentinels, lookouts—anyone whose function is to block the way of the hero or test his or her powers. Threshold guardians protect the secrets of a special world and can measure a hero's commitment and worth. Learning how to deal with threshold guardians is one of the major tests of the hero's journey.

BIBLE STORIES INVOLVING TESTS, TRIALS AND THRESHOLD GUARDIANS

Every Bible hero dealt with tests, trials and threshold guardians. Few came close to going through as much as Paul, the apostle who wrote most of the New Testament. Paul began as Saul of Tarsus, a highly educated and influential Jewish leader living at the time of Christ. Saul was deeply upset by the followers of Jesus of Nazareth, who insisted that Jesus had risen from the dead as predicted and thus proved his claims as Messiah. These Jewish followers of Jesus saw their new faith as an extension and fulfillment of Judaism. Little did Saul suspect that God was about to cause him to cross the threshold into the extraordinary world, where he would face innumerable tests, trials, challenges, tricksters and threshold guardians. Our story begins in Acts 9, after the execution of Stephen, the first martyr among Jesus' followers.

> Saul was still breathing out murderous threats against the Lord's disciples. He went to the high priest and asked him for letters to the synagogues in Damascus, so that if he found any there who belonged to the Way, whether men or women, he might take them as prisoners to Jerusalem.

Saul's horse galloped toward Damascus with his entourage when he met the greatest threshold guardian of all.

> As he neared Damascus on his journey, suddenly a light from heaven flashed around him. He fell to the ground and heard a voice say to him,
> "Saul, Saul, why do you persecute me?"
> "Who are you, Lord?" Saul asked.
> "I am Jesus, whom you are persecuting," he replied. "Now get up and go into the city, and you will be told what you must do." (Acts 9:1-6)

The men traveling with Saul stood there speechless; they heard the sound but didn't see anyone. Saul got up from the ground, blinded, and had to be led by the hand into Damascus—not exactly the entrance he planned. For three days he did not eat or drink. There in the dark, Saul realized he had not been playing on the hero team as he had supposed.

Meanwhile, the Lord presented a challenge to a disciple named Ananias who lived in Damascus. The Lord called to him in a vision and he answered. (Apparently he had already crossed the threshold into the extraordinary.) The Lord told him,

> Go to the house of Judas on Straight Street and ask for a man from Tarsus named Saul, for he is praying. In a vision he has seen a man named Ananias come and place his hands on him to restore his sight.

Ananias wasn't too keen to go to this man because of his reputation. He answered,

> "I have heard many reports about this man and all the harm he has done to your saints in Jerusalem. And he has come here with authority from the chief priests to arrest all who call on your name."
>
> But the Lord said to Ananias, "Go! This man is my chosen instrument to carry my name before the Gentiles and their kings and before the people of Israel. *I will show him how much he must suffer for my name.*"

So Ananias went to the house, placed his hands on Saul and said,

> Brother Saul, the Lord—Jesus, who appeared to you on the road as you were coming here—has sent me so that you may see again and be filled with the Holy Spirit. (Acts 9:11-17)

Ananias didn't mention how much Saul would have to suffer. He just prayed for Saul. Something like scales fell from Saul's eyes and he could see again. After crossing that threshold, there was no going back. He had seen the other world and the risen Jesus. He got up, was baptized and declared his allegiance to Jesus' hero team.

Saul now saw the Hebrew Scriptures in new light. Instead of going to the synagogues to incite them to round up Jesus' followers—as they expected—he showed up and announced himself the most recent convert. Instead of arresting Jesus' followers, he preached that Jesus is the Son of God. As one might guess, this didn't go over so well with the crowd.

> All those who heard him were astonished and asked, "Isn't he the man who raised havoc in Jerusalem among those who call on this name? And hasn't he come here to take them as prisoners to the chief priests?" Yet Saul grew more and more powerful and baffled the Jews living in Damascus by proving that Jesus is the Christ. (Acts 9:21-22)

It only took a matter of days before the Jews there conspired to kill him. He was stuck in a walled city with the most powerful men of that city determined to ambush him. They were literally threshold guardians, or perhaps the reverse since Paul is trying to get out. In the dark of night, however, Jesus' followers put Saul in a basket and lowered him through an opening in the wall. Their daring rescue succeeded, and Saul returned to Jerusalem.

Once in Jerusalem, Saul hoped to join Jesus' band of loyal followers. They didn't trust him (they thought he was a shapeshifter, which we'll discuss later), but Barnabas, nicknamed "the Son of Encouragement," stood up for him and got him past the threshold guardians to the inner circle, the apostles.

> He told them how Saul on his journey had seen the Lord and that the Lord had spoken to him, and how in Damascus he had preached fearlessly in the name of Jesus. So Saul stayed with them

and moved about freely in Jerusalem, speaking boldly in the name
of the Lord. (Acts 9:27-28)

Whew! He was now in, but the tests had just begun. Saul expanded
his audience to include Jews of Greek heritage; they tried to kill him too.
So his spiritual brothers took him to the nearest port, put him on a ship,
and sent him home to Tarsus. There he cooled his heels for more than a
decade; talk about developing patience!

Barnabas was in Antioch of Syria, where many non-Jewish people
(Gentiles) were coming to believe in Jesus. A prophet there predicted
that a great famine was about to hit the Roman world, so Barnabas was
appointed to take relief to Jerusalem. He called Saul to help him distribute relief aid. The disciples in Jerusalem were praying and fasting, seeking God fervently, when the Holy Spirit said, "Set apart for me Barnabas
and Saul for the work to which I have called them" (Acts 13:2). So, they
were sent off on their adventure (the first missionary journey).

They sailed to Cyprus, where they preached their way across the
island without interference. When they came to the city of Paphos, they
met the proconsul of the island, Sergius Paulus, and his attendant, Elymas. Elymas was a sorcerer—a trickster if ever there was one—who intended to distract his boss from their teaching, which might put him out
of business. Sometimes the best way to deal with a trickster or threshold
guardian is to make them into an ally, but other times they must be confronted, and Saul took the confrontational route here:

Saul, who was also called Paul, filled with the Holy Spirit, looked
straight at Elymas and said, "You are a child of the devil and an enemy of everything that is right! You are full of all kinds of deceit
and trickery. Will you never stop perverting the right ways of the
Lord? Now the hand of the Lord is against you. You are going to be
blind, and for a time you will be unable to see the light of the sun."
Immediately mist and darkness came over him, and he groped

about, seeking someone to lead him by the hand. When the pro-consul saw what had happened, he believed, for he was amazed at the teaching about the Lord. (Acts 13:9-12)

From here on out, Saul is called Paul.

Paul and Barnabas moved on to Perga where Paul preached a powerful sermon which was met with general approval. His reception among the people incited jealously among the Jewish religious leaders who opposed them, and they guarded their threshold by poisoning the minds of the crowds against them. Paul and Barnabas were given the power to confirm their message with signs and miraculous wonders, so the town was divided.

When Paul and Barnabas caught wind of a plot to stone them to death, they decided it was time to move on quickly. They fled to nearby towns, preaching to Gentiles instead of Jews. However, their former threshold guardians pursued them, incited a mob and ran Paul and Barnabas out of town. Not to be stopped, they went to the next town, Iconium, where opponents once again planned to stone them to death.

Given the mob hysteria that was building, they decided to run for their lives. So they went to the cities of Lystra and Derbe, where they preached and God empowered Paul to heal a handicapped man. Their Roman-influenced audience was familiar with Roman mythological figures and thought Paul must be Hermes and Barnabas, Zeus. While Paul and Barnabas were trying to dissuade the crowd from worshiping them, the outraged mob from Antioch and Iconium arrived, stoned Paul, dragged him from the city and left him for dead.

Death? Ha! Not quite yet. Paul had not completed his quest, so even death couldn't stop him. He got up and went back to all the cities where they had previously preached, strengthening the disciples and encouraging them to remain true to the faith. "We must go through many hardships"—that is to say, many trials, tests, and encounters with tricksters and threshold guardians –"to enter the kingdom of God," they said.

Paul's further journeys are an exciting continuation of tests, trials—including an actual trial for his life before Caesar—and challenges of many kinds. A letter to the church in Corinth recounts Paul's resume of tests, trials, challenges and all manner of threshold guardians and tricksters he had to overcome. "I have been," he recounts,

- beaten with rods three times
- stoned (with real stones)
- shipwrecked three times
- a night and a day adrift in the open sea
- constantly on the move
- in danger from rivers
- in danger from bandits
- in danger from my own countrymen
- in danger from Gentiles
- in danger in the city
- in danger in the country
- in danger at sea
- in danger from false brothers

Paul continued,

> I have labored and toiled and have often gone without sleep; I have known hunger and thirst and have often gone without food; I have been cold and naked. Besides everything else, I face daily the pressure of my concern for all the churches. (2 Corinthians 11:23-28)

Like any true hero, Paul did not let those tests, trials, challenges, tricksters, and threshold guardians keep him from reaching his purpose and the rightful conclusion to his hero's journey. While imprisoned for his faith, Paul wrote to the church at Philippi,

I want to know Christ and the power of his resurrection and the fellowship of sharing in his sufferings, becoming like him in his death, and so, somehow, to attain to the resurrection from the dead. Not that I have already obtained all this, or have already been made perfect, but I press on to take hold of that for which Christ Jesus took hold of me. Brothers, I do not consider myself yet to have taken hold of it. But one thing I do: Forgetting what is behind and straining toward what is ahead, I press on toward the goal to win the prize for which God has called me heavenward in Christ Jesus. All of us who are mature should take such a view of things. (Philippians 3:10-15)

So we see that, by the end of his life, Paul who began as Saul had become a true hero. He not only survived all the tests, trials, tricksters and threshold guardians, but he allowed the suffering and difficulties he encountered to toughen him up and mature him. Therefore, he could say that all who are mature should come to view life this way.

Everyone must go through tests, difficulties, struggles, temptations and trials. It's part of life, but we want to see some purpose behind it. God doesn't send tests, trial, challenges and threshold guardians to stop us, but to strengthen us. And we will need that strength because of the evil nature of our enemy, which we take up in the next chapter.

8

Knowing the Villain and the Nature of Evil

"Narnia is established. We must next take thought
for keeping it safe. . . . The world is not five hours old
and an evil has already entered it."

Aslan, The Magician's Nephew

Every great fantasy story must have its villain, usually one supreme enemy who is dedicated to the hero's death and destruction of the good. The villain serves the dramatic role of a worthy opponent who challenges the hero team, creates ongoing conflict and requires the heroes to fight back, thus bringing out the best in them. Villains are unrelenting; therefore, the villain and forces of evil must be recognized and vanquished if the hero is to fulfill his or her quest.

All three of our stories have excellently drawn villains: *Harry Potter* has Voldemort; *Star Wars* has Darth Sidius and Darth Vader. In Narnia we meet several villains, most notably the White Witch—formerly Jadis, Queen of Charn, who enslaves Narnia in perpetual winter and turns her foes into stone. In *The Silver Chair* we see the Lady of the Green Kirtle, who murdered Prince Rilian's mother, kidnapped and enslaved him. In *Prince Caspian* there is King Miraz, the usurper, and *The Last Battle* presents a villain team. All three of our stories use the ancient symbol of the serpent in association with evil. In *Harry Potter* it is the image associated with Slytherin, the house from which Voldemort came, also the Basilisk, King of Snakes, and Nagini. In *Star Wars: The Empire Strikes Back* we see a serpent in a tree as Luke walks slowly into the mist to face the image of Darth Vader. In Narnia we see the Lady of the Green Kirtle transform into a deadly serpent.

The villain is a dramatic personification of evil: all our villains are murderous, killing anyone—even whole worlds full of people—to achieve their aims. They are usurpers, thieves, deceivers, rebellious and arrogant; they use terror and fear of death to control others. They are accusers, slanderers and abusers. All are aggressively on the move to achieve their evil aims. By personalizing and dramatizing the nature of evil in our villains, we can learn to recognize evil characteristics and better guard against evil in our world and—as Aslan said—"take thought for keeping it safe."

Evil is a corruption of the good, a perversion rather than a new creation. In the course of a fantastic story, we can learn from villains as well as heroes. We can watch the effect of evil over the course of time, following characters as they descend down into evil, struggle against it or work on its behalf. We can see the progression that led a character to become evil, what happens as that character is enveloped by evil and the consequences of taking such a path. Let's start by looking at what the Bible has to say about evil, and then see how our villains measure up to evil of biblical proportions.

The Nature of Evil as Revealed in the Bible

Villains in fantastic stories are spiritually useful to the degree that they exemplify biblical truths about the nature of evil and how to protect against it. The table on page 124 gives a general overview of the nature of evil as identified in the Bible (to large degree, the opposite of God's goodness). These are not simply evil archetypes but how the Bible identifies the evil one. The table also shows the Bible references, specific behavior

Nature	Scripture	Behavior	Outcome	Example
Murderous A murderer	John 10:10 Hebrews 2:14 1 Peter 5:8 Matthew 7:15	Comes to kill Holds power of death Seeks to devour Ferocious, ravenous	Murders Loss & death Fear Terror	Voldemort Darth Sidius Darth Vader Lady of the Green Kirtle
Deceiver / Liar Father of Lies Perverse / Crooked	Matthew 7:15 2 Cor. 11:14-15 John 8:44	Masquerades as good Doesn't speak straight Lies and has others lie	Deception People misled Truth hidden	Prof. Quirrell Darth Sidius White Witch
Rebel Rebellious Arrogant	Rev. 12:7-9 Genesis 3 Isaiah 59: 1-3	Led rebellion of angels Led people to disobey Stirs up dissension	Lawlessness Wars, guilt, loss Dissension	Tom Riddle Anakin Skywalker Jadis of Charn
Discourager Fear monger	Nehemiah 4:1-23 2 Kings 18:19-35 Hebrew 2:15	Discouragement Intimidation Terrorist tactics	Weakness Giving up People in terror Enslaved by fear	Prof. Umbrage Emperor White Witch King Miraz
Accuser Slanderer	Job 2:1 Rev. 12:10 Proverbs 16:28	Hurls accusations Slanders innocent Stirs up gossip	Injustice People hurt Friends separated	Rita Skeeter Darth Sidius White Witch
Abuser	Psalm 55:9-11 Job 2:7 Luke 22:3 Matthew 27:5	Misuses people Likes inflicting pain Others do dirty work then are discarded	People used for evil Torture Pain & suffering Loss & regrets	Voldemort White Witch Darth Sidius Darth Vader
Aggressor	Hebrews 2:14 2 Corinthians 2:11 Ephesians 6:11	On the prowl plotting	Great danger if we do not remain alert	Voldemort Jadis of Charn Darth Sidius

associated with that aspect of evil, outcomes of evildoing and characters in our stories who exemplify that characteristic.

KNOWING THE VILLAINS IN HARRY POTTER

In the villain of *Harry Potter and the Chamber of Secrets* we see the budding *murderous* nature of evil: the memory of Tom Riddle (young Voldemort) is awakened in his enchanted diary. As a student he sought to kill mudbloods, loosing the Basilisk that killed Moaning Myrtle. He destroyed Hagrid's reputation, and marred his future by framing him and falsely accusing him of releasing the monster. He possessed Ginny. He sought to destroy Dumbledore's authority and Hogwarts along with it. He reveled in death and held the entire wizarding world in fear of the Avada Kedavra curse. Recall the enjoyment Tom Riddle took in watching Harry die from the venom of the Basilisk and you have a vivid portrait of evil. This murderous nature of evil is similarly depicted by Fenrir Greyback, the bloodthirsty werewolf who delights in ferociously attacking children, and by the very name Death Eaters: by their very nature, they feed on death, and they were known to kill and torture for fun when Voldemort was in power. These villains have utter disregard for life. Voldemort thinks nothing of murdering whoever interferes in his quest, even his own ancestors. When Harry and Cedric are dragged into a graveyard in *Harry Potter and the Goblet of Fire,* Voldemort tells his associates to "kill the spare," not even acknowledging Harry's companion as a person. *Harry Potter and the Order of the Phoenix* reminds us that many members of the hero team were murdered by Death Eaters.

We see the *deceptive* nature of evil in *Harry Potter and the Sorcerer's Stone*. Professor Quirrell is a deceiver, pretending to befriend Harry while letting the troll in and plotting to steal the Sorcerer's Stone, kill Harry and destroy Hogwarts. As Defense against the Dark Arts teacher, he pretended to be shy and sheepish; but was a wolf in sheep's clothing. Barty Crouch Jr. also deceived everyone as Professor Moody in *Harry*

Potter and the Goblet of Fire, tricking Harry to think of him as a friend while plotting his murder. Professor Lockhart gilded himself in coiffed hair, brilliant robes, feigned exploits, and a sparkling smile; but his shining appearance hid a darkly selfish heart. His fraud almost cost Ginny her life in *Harry Potter and the Chamber of Secrets*. Not recognizing these deceptions early enough endangers those on the side of good. In all these characters, we learn a great lesson in dealing with evil: don't be surprised if it is disguised to look as close to that which is good as possible.

The nature of evil is *rebellious* and *arrogant*. Villains see themselves not as "villains" but as heroes of their own myths. Tom Riddle longed to go beyond what he could learn at Hogwarts to delve into the forbidden Dark Arts, and went further than any wizard in pursuing immortality, although it shattered his soul. Consider how differently Professor Quirrell saw what he was doing from how the reader, Harry and Dumbledore saw it. Quirrell mocks the "ridiculous ideas about good and evil" from his youth. "Lord Voldemort showed me how wrong I was. There is no good and evil, there is only power, and those too weak to seek it."

Evil *causes fear and discouragement*. Consider the fear shown by Voldemort's followers as well as his enemies. Look at how Dementors suck happiness and hope from those they come near, leaving them with only their most terrible memories. Villains cause fear, discouragement, and dishearten everyone, as with Delores Umbrage, who does her utmost to discourage Harry from becoming an auror.

It is in the nature of evil to *accuse and slander.* Rita Skeeter's slanderous stories cause great harm, and twisted reports in the *Daily Prophet* demean Dumbledore and Harry, and hurt the cause of good. The gossip at Hogwarts hurts Harry, and the false accusations hurled at Sirius Black, Hagrid and Dumbledore unleash destructive power.

The nature of evil is *abusive*. Dumbledore observes of Voldemort in *Sorcerer's Stone,* "He left Quirrell to die; he shows just as little mercy to his followers as to his enemies." When I read that I think of Judas Iscariot; when Satan was done using him, Judas died a terrible death at his own hand. Even though both Judas and Quirrell chose the wrong path, their end reveals that their evil masters offered them no mercy. Evil enjoys inflicting pain; those loyal to Voldemort readily use the torturous Cruciatis curse, but when Harry tries it on Bellatrix Lestrange, she tells him that righteous indignation is not enough to activate it; one has to *enjoy* inflicting pain.

The nature of evil is *aggressive*. Even when not in power, Voldemort is scheming, murdering and actively plotting to regain his body and overthrow the rightful authorities. He, like all well-drawn villains, is never passive, even behind the scenes. Tom Riddle started out with the same potential for good or evil with his magical powers as any other Hogwarts student; he aggressively *chose* the dark path, believing it would give him more power. Dumbledore saw his descent into darkness as a choice to pursue darkness.

INNOCENCE OVERTAKEN BY EVIL

Young, naive, careless and needy, Ginny Weasley is overtaken and possessed by evil in *Harry Potter and the Chamber of Secrets*. She finds a suspicious diary and discovers that it soothes her loneliness. Tom Riddle presents himself to her through his enchanted diary and, by telling her what she wants to hear, gets her to confide in him and open herself to his influence for his own evil, unsuspected designs.

Riddle laughed, a high, cold laugh that didn't suit him. It made the hairs stand up on the back of Harry's neck.

"If I say it myself, Harry, I've always been able to charm the people I needed. So Ginny poured out her soul to me, and her soul happened to be exactly what I wanted. . . . I grew stronger and stronger on a diet of her deepest fears, her darkest secrets. I grew powerful, far more powerful than little Miss Weasley. Powerful enough to start feeding Miss Weasley a few of *my* secrets, to start pouring a little of *my* soul back into her."

When her parents finally learn what Ginny has done by trusting the diary, her father chides her for not showing the diary to him or her mother since it was clearly full of Dark Magic. "Haven't I taught you *anything*? What have I always told you? Never trust anything that can think for itself *if you can't see where it keeps its brain?*"

As a parent, I can't help thinking how crucial Mr. Weasley's advice is for everyone who communicates over the Internet on social networking sites and in chat rooms. There are evildoers using the Internet to lure needy people into their schemes. We must warn our children about pouring out their soul to anyone they communicate with but don't really know. Evil is predatory and deceptive; therefore we would do well to heed Mr. Weasley's warning. Any time we sense that we need to hide something from those we know have our best interests at heart—those committed to our good—evil is probably lurking therein.

KNOWING THE VILLAINS IN NARNIA

Throughout the Chronicles of Narnia, murder, destruction and greed are the marks of Aslan's enemies. We see the *murderous* nature of evil depicted in the wolves loyal to the White Witch, who seek to kill the children. Miraz in *Prince Caspian* kills his brother, the rightful king, and his consorts to make himself king. In *The Silver Chair* the Lady of the Green Kirtle is the snake who kills Prince Rilian's mother, robs him of his freedom and plots to overthrow Narnia.

We see the *deceptive* nature of evil in the way the White Witch portrays herself as Queen of Narnia and pretends to care for Edmund. The Lady of the Green Kirtle similarly deceives Prince Rilian and fools Eustace, Jill and Puddleglum into taking refuge with the "Gentle Giants" of Harfang, who plan to eat them. The grand deception is planned by Shift the ape, who tries to pass off a donkey wearing a lion skin as Aslan.

We see *rebellion and arrogance* in Jadis, the White Witch. She comes to Narnia's creation from another world, which she has destroyed. She climbs a wall into a garden to steal fruit from the Tree of Protection. Jadis makes herself a rival to any who would rule, including all the coming kings and queens of Narnia and Aslan himself. In Jadis and Uncle Andrew we see the rebellious spirit personified. They regard themselves as above any law, able to do as they please, arrogantly going beyond limitations set for the common good. When Digory calls Uncle Andrew "rotten" for breaking his promise, he explains,

> But, of course you must understand that rules of that sort, however excellent they may be for little boys—and servants—and women—and even people in general, can't possibly be expected to apply to profound students and great thinkers and sages. No, Digory. Men like me who possess hidden wisdom, are freed from common rules.

All the villains of Narnia spread *fear and discouragement*. The White Witch holds all Narnia under her control by threatening to turn creatures into stone. Miraz holds his kingdom in fear. The underlanders rejoice to be free of the fear and discouragement which shrouded their lives under the rule of the Lady of the Green Kirtle.

We also see that the White Witch is an *accuser.* She brings an accusation against Edmund, even though his offense is not against her. She insists on the death penalty as punishment for his treachery. She is also *abusive,* whipping her dwarf and abusing Edmund when he returns to her. We see her *aggressive* nature revealed from the moment she escapes Charn, still known as Jadis. Regardless of what world she enters, she is intent upon becoming the unquestioned ruler, as she demonstrates in her rampage through London and her declaration of herself to be the queen of Narnia.

When Jadis was queen of Charn, she hardened her heart to the point that she had no compassion for anyone in her world, even her own sister. Knowing that the Deplorable Word would destroy Charn, she used it to spite her sister and prolong her chance at ultimate power. When Digory and Polly awaken her, using the enchanted bell and hammer she left for that purpose, she is already intent on conquering other worlds—whether our world or another matters little. Therefore, when she enters newly created Narnia, Aslan rightly predicts that evil is ingrained in her; if given a chance she will work her evil there. Therefore, he determines that she must be opposed. The Tree of Protection covers Narnia for some time, but when Jadis gains power as the White Witch, the only way to deal with her is to destroy her.

We learn here that ingrained evil projects itself into whatever situation is presented to it, and it must be opposed by active forces of good. Adolf Hitler was intent on imposing Nazi rule on all of Europe and eventually the world. The conflict against confirmed evil comes with great risk, but the risk is greater if evil is not opposed. Those battling evil must be well prepared and willing to act or all could be lost. Action need not be violent; Gandhi and Martin Luther King Jr. are both examples of those who dared to take nonviolent action to resist evil. However, evil can only be overcome by *active* forces of good. Winston Churchill said, "I never worry about action, but only inaction." If the side of good waits too long, self-defense may be the only option.

KNOWING THE VILLAINS IN *STAR WARS*

In the first three movies in the *Star Wars* series, Darth Sidius is the great villain. He lures Anakin Skywalker from being a Jedi Knight to the dark side, actively scheming to make him his apprentice. He is disguised at first as Senator Palpatine, eventually becoming Chancellor and then Emperor. His evil designs and lust for power are not satisfied until he has total control over the galaxy and every Jedi is destroyed. Darth Sidius recruits, seduces and damages Anakin, shaping him into Darth Vader, who becomes the primary villain for the remaining three movies. Luke must face and conquer him to become a full fledged Jedi Master.

In the *Star Wars* series we see the *murderous* nature of evil when the Emperor and Darth Vader, along with the forces of the Empire, set out to achieve domination with the ultimate weapon, the Death Star. They do not hesitate to destroy an entire planet without pity for Princess Leia, who loves the people of that world. Those on the side of the Empire are indiscriminate killers, eliminating even those on their own side whose performance disappoints them and commanding the killing of innocent children. The Emperor, for example, initiates Anakin Skywalker by having him violate the Jedi Code, killing everyone at the Jedi Temple, even the innocent younglings.

We see the *deceptiveness* of evil in the way Darth Sidius disguises himself as a respectable member of society, but also in how he lures Anakin to the dark side. He acts as though he cares whether Padmé lives through the birth of their children, thus getting Anakin to make the bargain to come over to the dark side in order to be empowered to stop death. All of this was a deception. Once Anakin is in too deep to get out—after he kills the younglings—Darth Sidius does nothing to save Padmé.

In Anakin Skywalker we see the *rebelliousness and arrogance* of evil. This weakness was present from a young age and was the weakness Darth Sidius used to draw him in. When Anakin's mother dies, Padmé comments that no one could stop death, but Anakin thinks he should have been powerful enough, should have been able to make her live. He vows that some day he will gain power over death. His arrogance also shows up when he is not made a Jedi Master after the Chancellor insists he be put on the Jedi Council. He feels rebellious toward the council and Obi-Wan Kenobi when he has to stay behind while Obi-Wan is sent on an important mission. This rebellious streak is encouraged by Darth Sidius because it gives him a foothold in Anakin's life.

Darth Sidius, known as the Emperor, and Darth Vader bring *fear* on all those under their command, killing anyone who doesn't perform up to their standards. Their nonchalance and sense of calm while strangling or electrocuting their own people with the dark side of the force chills all in their presence.

We see Darth Sidius get Anakin to commit atrocities when he first turns to the dark side, and the *accusations* and true guilt for such gross evil deeds make it impossible for Anakin to go back to being a Jedi. We see *abusiveness* in how Darth Sidius allows Anakin to be dragged into a fiery pit, partially dismembered, and marred terribly before encasing him in the mechanized frame that becomes universally recognized as Darth Vader.

The *aggressive* nature of evil plays out in the elaborate plans carried out by the Empire to create a weapon that could destroy entire planets, thus giving them the power to enslave the entire galaxy. When Luke resists the Emperor's invitation to join the dark side, a terrible sense of delight flickers across the face of the Emperor as he electrocutes Luke. We should remember the look of that face, and call it to mind any time we start to think of evil as anything less than terrible.

FROM GOOD TO EVIL

How Anakin Skywalker digresses from a good Jedi to the villainous Darth Vader was the main advertising hook for *Star Wars: The Revenge of the Sith*. Promotional materials promised that all questions about Darth Vader's creation would be answered. The hero's journey of Anakin Skywalker, including his digression into the villainous journey of Darth Vader, is worthy of attention in its own right. Before Luke and Leia were even a gleam in their father's eye, Anakin was the hope of the Jedi Knights. He was talented and full of promise. Obi-Wan Kenobi saw his potential and trained him. However, the Emperor saw Anakin's potential too, and coveted it for the dark side. If only Anakin had recognized that his fears were not reality and that someone given over to the dark side could not be trusted to spare Padmé's life, how different his journey would have been! When Anakin believed the lies of the evil one, and was lured to cross over to the dark side—albeit for "good" reason—he became the instrument of Padmé's death. The Emperor had him without entanglements of love, filled with guilt, self-reproach and anger; Anakin was empty, open for evil to permeate his being. Thus he became Darth Vader. We would do well to consider all these small steps that made him vulnerable and his mistakes in judgment, so as to avoid similar ones.

However, Darth Vader was not entirely lost, as we shall see in chapter fourteen. In fantastic stories, as in life, there is hope even for those apparently consumed by evil.

The Bible says that we contend against an evil villain, one who existed before our world was created but entered it shortly after. This evil one works through forces of darkness in the spiritual realm. As the villains in our fantastic stories are personalities, so too the Bible says that evil in our world is influenced by an evil *one*. He is not the evil opposite of God, as some mistakenly conceive of him, but rather a former angel who once worshiped God but in arrogance made himself God's rival. Thus the evil one in the Bible is the opposite of a good angel. When he was cast out of heaven for his rebellion against the Most High, he took one third of the angels with him. Their rebellion was already in progress when God created Adam and Eve, and carries on to this day. These dark spiritual influences are our opponents in our battles. Ephesians 6:12 explains, "For our struggle is not against flesh and blood, but against the rulers, against the authorities, against the powers of this dark world and against the spiritual forces of evil in the heavenly realms."

The Bible reveals that "the evil one" in our world is Satan—the devil, Lucifer, described as a dragon or serpent and also known as "the god of this world" and "prince of the powers of the air." He has designs for our destruction. Therefore, we must be aware of the kinds of schemes he would devise. When Paul wrote to the church at Corinth he told them to be obedient to God and to forgive, "in order that Satan might not out-wit us. For we are not unaware of his schemes" (2 Corinthians 2:11).

The characteristics on the table on page 124 are also seen in the spiritual forces of darkness the Bible warns us against. By keeping these in mind, we can remain sober about the nature of our opponent and be better able to defend against his evil attacks on us and our loved ones.

Evil is *murderous*. Jesus said false prophets were "inwardly like ravenous wolves." Jesus described those on the side of evil as coming with three purposes: to "steal, kill, and destroy" (John 10:10).

According to the Bible, the nature of the evil one is *deceptive*. Jesus called him "a liar and the father of lies." The Bible also says that the devil masquerades as "an angel of light," doesn't speak straight, hides the truth, misleads people and is perverse.

The evil one is inherently *rebellious*. Satan led a rebellion of angels against God. Revelation 12:7-9 says,

> And there was war in heaven. Michael and his angels fought against the dragon, and the dragon and his angels fought back. But he was not strong enough, and they lost their place in heaven. The great dragon was hurled down—that ancient serpent called the devil, or Satan, who leads the whole world astray. He was hurled to the earth, and his angels with him.

We should also note that the forces of evil were not strong enough to win that battle against the forces of God. Satan led one third of the angels after him, fallen angels that became demons. However, simple arithmetic reminds us that two thirds of the angels remained on God's side; so the fallen angels are outnumbered two to one, and God is far more powerful than Satan.

We see the *arrogance* of Satan in a passage from the prophet Isaiah that describes Lucifer's downfall. As you read it, consider how differently he views himself than God viewed his rebellion:

How you have fallen from heaven,
    O morning star [Lucifer], son of the dawn!
You have been cast down to the earth,
    you who once laid low the nations!
You said in your heart,
    "I will ascend to heaven;
I will raise my throne
    above the stars of God;
I will sit enthroned on the mount of assembly,
    on the utmost heights of the sacred mountain.
I will ascend above the tops of the clouds;
    I will make myself like the Most High."
But you are brought down to the grave,
    to the depths of the pit.

Those who see you stare at you,
    they ponder your fate:
"Is this the man who shook the earth?" (Isaiah 14:12-16)

Indeed, true evil has shaken the earth. Think of anyone who is recognized by their nature and deeds as being evil, someone like Adolf Hitler, who openly turned to the occult and was thought by many, even in his inner circle, to be demon-possessed. Think of the way his murderous, deceitful, rebellious, arrogant, terrorist, abusive, aggressive nature, evil plans and deeds literally shook the earth. Even though Satan has been cast down, we are still shaken by the influence of evil when it is unbridled and working through people who yield themselves to the dark side rather than to God. God has given those on his side power and authority to thwart the evil one and his dark schemes; but that power must be exercised. To do so, we must first recognize that evil does exist and has a profound impact on the world in which we live. This is in keeping with what Hebrews 2:14 says, that the devil "holds the power of death" and holds people enslaved by fear of death.

The evil one we must contend with is truly *diabolical,* a word that orig-inates from *diabolos,* Greek for "accuser" or "slanderer." This aspect of evil greatly impacts people and their relationship to God. If Satan can con-vince us that we are not good enough, or are too sinful, by accusing us of our real sins, then we may stay distant from God, which is precisely what Satan wants. One scene in the Bible gives us a peek into the courts of heaven when Satan came before God to accuse his righteous servant, Job.

> On another day the angels came to present themselves before the LORD, and Satan also came with them to present himself before him. And the LORD said to Satan, "Where have you come from?"
>
> Satan answered the LORD, "From roaming through the earth and going back and forth in it."
>
> Then the LORD said to Satan, "Have you considered my servant Job? There is no one on earth like him; he is blameless and upright, a man who fears God and shuns evil. And he still maintains his in-tegrity, though you incited me against him to ruin him without any reason." (Job 2:1-3)

Satan made *slanderous* accusations against Job, saying that if his life took a terrible turn—one that Satan would gladly cause to happen—Job would curse God. The Lord allowed Satan to test Job. He is the same one who accuses us, and heaps on condemnation, seeking to separate us from God by shame and guilt.

In Revelation 12:10 we see that when the power of the kingdom of God is fully established, "the accuser" will be hurled down. It says he was the one who accused those on God's side before Him, day and night. So that inclination to slander and accuse is characteristic of evil. On an earthly level, we have all experienced the pain of being gossiped about, slandered, spoken ill of or accused because of our sins. It tears us down, which is a primary aim of Satan.

The nature of the evil one is seriously *aggressive*. First Peter 5:8 says, "Your enemy the devil prowls around like a roaring lion looking for someone to devour." He is on the move, seeking to devour, destroy and kill. Just as we would never want to be unarmed facing a hungry lion hunting for a kill, likewise we should be well armed to face aggressive evil on the prowl in our world.

FACE TO FACE WITH EVIL

What can we learn by our look at the nature of evil as revealed in the Bible and exemplified in the stories of *Star Wars,* Narnia and Harry Potter? Knowing the nature of evil and being able to recognize it allows us to effectively oppose it. The Bible gives us a basic stance to take when confronted with evil:

- You "who love the LORD, hate evil!" (Psalm 97:10)
- "Hate what is evil; cling to what is good." (Romans 12:9)
- "Do not be overcome evil, but overcome evil with good." (Romans 12:21)

When Jesus was on earth, demons trembled in his presence, and the Bible assures us in 1 John 4:4 that Christ, the Holy Spirit—"he who is in you"— is greater "than he who is in the world" (Satan). So we are to hate evil, overcome it with good and remember that for those on God's side, our power—God's power in us is greater than the power of evil.

The Bible says, "Resist the devil and he will flee from you" (James 4:7). By resisting evil, firm in faith, we activate God's power to thwart evil. Knowing the nature of evil, hating it, opposing it and overcoming evil with good are essential to our life's fulfillment.

Given the deceptiveness of evil we can't always recognize it easily. This is especially true when those on the side of evil play the shapeshifter in order to deceive. We'll look at shapeshifters in our next chapter.

9

Unveiling Shapeshifters in Our Fight Against Evil

"This is not Alastor Moody," said Dumbledore quietly. "You have never known Alastor Moody. The real Moody would not have removed you from my sight after what happened tonight. The moment he took you, I knew—and followed."

Dumbledore to Harry, Harry Potter and the Goblet of Fire

Shapeshifters are classic character types in fantasy fiction. Shapeshifters are not what they appear to be; some can change their physical form, as an animagus does in the Harry Potter series. They may change, like a werewolf, with the phases of the moon.

Shapeshifters develop suspense and create doubt, leaving the hero (and reader or viewer) to wonder if that character is an ally or an enemy, and if the shapeshifter is adept at concealment, the hero may not even wonder. Shapeshifters are not always evil characters pretending to be good; they may be mentors or allies who change appearance or misrepresent themselves in order to help the hero. From the hero's point of view, shapeshifters may seem two-faced or difficult to pin down; they are misrepresenting themselves to someone, but to whom? Their loyalty and sincerity may be in question by both sides. That's the thing about shape-shifters, we're just not sure. With patience the hero will eventually find out the truth, but whether or not the hero team trusts a shapeshifter impacts how the story plays out.

The shapeshifter depicts our human condition. In life there are people who are not what they present themselves to be, or who are more than what we can see. We don't know what is in the hearts of others. We don't know who can be trusted, and we're not sure how to handle others who present themselves falsely. If we entrust ourselves to one given over to evil, we may be hurt or used for that person's selfish aims. We also need to identify spiritual forces and entities that are known to represent themselves falsely; Satan, the Bible tells us, masquerades as an angel of light. We also need to recognize, however, that at times God shows up in an unexpected form. Our personal and spiritual well-being is influenced by whether we can recognize shapeshifters and deal with them appropriately.

FALSE FRONTS

In *The Lion, the Witch and the Wardrobe,* the White Witch presents herself to Edmund as Queen of Narnia—a title she has no legal right to hold. She feigns kindness to Edmund and promises him a position as prince in her kingdom. Meanwhile she is plotting to destroy him and his brother and sisters, keeping them from becoming the rightful rulers of Narnia, as Aslan intended. Her kindness covers cold, calculating evil. Her lies, usurpation and murderous intent are covered up with the false sweetness of enchanted Turkish Delight, Edmund's favorite candy.

In *Star Wars: The Empire Strikes Back,* even Han Solo isn't sure whether Lando Calrissian is friend or foe when they reunite in Cloud City. After a moment of play acting (which alerts the audience that he might not be what he seems), Lando presents himself as a friend. He acts friendly enough, offering to have the Millennium Falcon repaired and providing hospitality to Han, Leia, Chewbacca, C-3PO and R2-D2. But Leia doesn't trust him, and we later learn that he has put up a false front. Unbeknownst to the hero team, Lando has struck a deal with Darth Vader, who arrived shortly before the Millennium Falcon. Under pressure from the Empire, Lando agrees to set up Han and hand over those with him.

So, Lando is on the evil side, right? Not so fast. He is also a shapeshifter to the Empire. While acting as a traitor to the hero team, apparently because of self-interest, he implements a plan to rescue them and manages to take off in the Millennium Falcon with Leia, Chewbacca, C-3PO and R2-D2. At great risk to himself, he goes back to rescue Luke from the antenna of Cloud City. Throughout this episode and *Return of the Jedi*, Lando is shifty, showing up in disguise, leaving us unsure about him as the story unfolds. He's a shapeshifter, even though he doesn't change his physical form.

Shapeshifters that *can* change physical form leave the hero team cautious about who's who and what the characters *really* are. In *The Silver Chair,* the lovely Lady of the Green Kirtle presents herself as Queen of the Underworld. On the surface, she has a kind and loving relationship with Rilian, whom she adopted and promised to make a prince once he helps her overthrow those in the overworld. However, we discover that she was the poisonous green snake who murdered Rilian's mother, a true queen, so that she could kidnap Prince Rilian and use him for her evil plot. The silver chair, for which the story is named, is presented as a protection for Rilian, a restraint against madness. However, it actually restrains him from discovering his rightful place in Aslan's kingdom.

Jill, Eustace and Puddleglum destroy the silver chair and free Rilian. Suddenly the Lady of the Green Kirtle arrives and, as the White Witch had done using Turkish Delight, uses enchanted sweetness to try to hold her prey. She keeps her beautiful form, puts a perfumed powder into the fire and plays sweet music, all the while trying to drive from their minds all remembrance of the true life in the overworld. When her enchantments are stamped out by Puddleglum, and their ability to see things truly is restored, she takes her true form, becoming a serpent and attempting to crush Rilian before having her head hacked off by him, Puddleglum and Eustace. Their failure to recognize the Lady of the Green Kirtle for what she truly was almost cost Rilian his life and his rightful place in the kingdom of Narnia.

Harry Potter encounters an abundance of shapeshifters, both those who change physical form and those who appear to change loyalties. A few times in *Prisoner of Azkaban,* even the reader isn't sure who is whom, or who is on the side of the hero team. The Grim, a great black dog thought to be an omen of death, appears to Harry; only later do we find out the Grim is Sirius Black in the form of his animagus. But isn't Sirius Black the mass murderer who betrayed Harry's parents? It turns out he was their faithful friend and Harry's godfather. He appears near Harry in order to unveil the *other* shapeshifter, Scabbers—Ron Weasley's pet rat—who turns out to be Peter Pettigrew, the traitor who revealed the whereabouts of Harry's parents. So the one thought to be evil and murderous turns out to be good, while the supposedly harmless pet is unveiled as responsible for multiple murders. Talk about shapeshifter whiplash!

Professor Severus Snape is a classic shapeshifter. Throughout the Harry Potter series he acts as though he hates Harry but his actions require the reader (and the hero team) to consider whether this might be put on for effect. In *Sorcerer's Stone* Harry and friends suspect Snape as the villain up until the final scene, when they discover that he saved Harry's life. As one reads the series it's hard to stay settled on whether Snape is on the side of good or evil. Snape is mistrusted by both sides: Belatrix Lastrange of the Death Eaters doesn't trust him and neither do some in the Order of the Phoenix. Even at the end of book six, when Professor Snape commits a terrible act, the reader and characters in the story are left to wonder: why does Dumbledore plead, "Please, Severus . . ." Is he asking Snape to do what he does in the end—for some unknown reason to be revealed in the final installment? Or is he pleading for Snape not to do it? In the great battle at the end of Harry's sixth year in *Half-Blood Prince,* why does Snape stop the Death Eaters from torturing Harry with the Cruciatis Curse? Why does he deflect the curses from the Order of the Phoenix fighters rather than retaliate? Snape leaves us wondering.

THE INTENTION OF THE HEART

Why does a person become a shapeshifter? Are they deceiving in order to destroy? Are they overpowered by evil? Are they consumed with shame and protecting themselves from the consequences of wrong-doing? If only we could know the intentions of the heart!

In the Harry Potter series we see recurrent ploys where shapeshifters deceive in order to destroy. Quirrell pretends to be Harry's friend and a teacher of Defense against the Dark Aarts. He deceives Hagrid to discover how to get past Fluffy to the Sorcerer's Stone so he can help Voldemort return to power. In *Chamber of Secrets* the deceptive nature of Tom Riddle's diary seduces Ginny Weasley and deceives Harry, who believes that Hagrid originally released the monster from the chamber.

Tom Riddle plays the shapeshifter with the purpose to destroy. Some, however, take on a shapeshifer persona for less malevolent reasons. Ginny hides evidence of her complicity in loosing the monster of the Heir of Slytherin. She acts out of shame and fear, having been overpowered by evil. Gilderoy Lockhart takes on a false front out of arrogance; his reckless disregard for others as he attempts to protect a persona of perfection hurts many people and almost costs Ginny, Ron and Harry their lives.

The shapeshifter's true nature and the intentions of their hearts are revealed as the story plays out. Those whose predisposition toward the side of good has been temporarily overpowered by evil, such as Lando Calrissian, Ginny Weasley and Prince Rilian, are redeemed. Those intending to destroy—such as the White Witch, the Lady of the Green

Kirtle and Professor Quirrell—are eventually exposed and punished. With shapeshifters abounding, we have to be cautious but give characters—and people we know—the benefit of the doubt until we see how their lives play out.

A STRATEGY OF STEALTH

Fantastic stories occasionally show the good side using stealth to oppose evil. The Defense Association (Dumbledore's Army) hides their secret training sessions in *Harry Potter and the Order of the Phoenix*. Remus Lupin lives among the werewolves in order to spy on them for Dumbledore. Lupin deceives, but not to destroy; his deception is used to protect the freedom and security of innocent people threatened by the Death Eaters. This is similar to undercover police who disguise themselves as criminals, doing and saying things to gain the trust of those whose wrongdoing they are trying to stop. Winston Churchill said of the resistance forces using deceptive means to stay alive and fight the Nazis in World War II: "In wartime, truth is so precious that she should always be attended by a bodyguard of lies."

This, of course, leaves people involved in battles between good and evil not quite sure who to trust. So what does the Bible have to say about shapeshifters in real life? Jesus taught his disciples to

> watch out for false prophets. They come to you in sheep's clothing, but inwardly they are ferocious wolves. By their fruit you will recognize them. Do people pick grapes from thornbushes, or figs from thistles? Likewise every good tree bears good fruit, but a bad tree bears bad fruit. A good tree cannot bear bad fruit, and a bad tree cannot bear good fruit. Every tree that does not bear good fruit is cut down and thrown into the fire. Thus, by their fruit you will recognize them. (Matthew 7:15-20)

The actions of the character and what emanates from his or her life over the course of time (as fruit grows from the tree) shows the true nature of the source. At the end of *Harry Potter and the Goblet of Fire,* Dumbledore tells Harry to stay put after he returns from the graveyard with Cedric's body. But "Professor Moody" removes Harry to his office. That act of disobedience convinces Dumbledore that Moody is an imposter.

SHAPESHIFTING IN THE BIBLE

Shapeshifters take a central role in many Bible stories. As a young man, Jacob—a patriarch of the Jewish and Christian faiths—disguised himself as his elder brother Esau in order to trick his father into giving him the birthright and blessing intended for his brother. He did this with the full cooperation of his mother. When Esau vowed to kill him, Jacob's mother sent him to her relatives, where one shapeshifter on the run learned from a master deceiver, his uncle Laban.

Laban had two daughters, Leah and Rachel. Jacob fell in love with Rachel (the younger daughter) and made a deal with Laban: Jacob would work for him seven years; in exchange, Rachel would become his wife. Laban switched the sisters before the wedding, however, so that the one hidden under the veil was not Rachel but her older sister, Leah. After the marriage was consummated (one does wonder how much wine he drank) Jacob awoke with the wrong woman in his bed. Shifty Uncle Laban excused himself by saying their custom did not allow the younger sister to wed before the elder. However, if Jacob would commit to seven more years of service, he could have Rachel also—immediately—as a second wife.

Fast forward thirteen years. God sent Jacob and his growing family back to his homeland where Jacob had to face Esau. Heading back, he was confronted one night by "a man" or an "angel of the Lord" or the Lord in the form of an angel or a man. Here is the account of this most mysterious of Bible encounters:

So Jacob was left alone, and a man wrestled with him till daybreak. When the man saw that he could not overpower him, he touched the socket of Jacob's hip so that his hip was wrenched as he wrestled with the man. Then the man said, "Let me go, for it is daybreak."

But Jacob replied, "I will not let you go unless you bless me."

The man asked him, "What is your name?"

"Jacob," he answered.

Then the man said, "Your name will no longer be Jacob, but Israel, because you have struggled with God and with men and have overcome."

Jacob said, "Please tell me your name."

But he replied, "Why do you ask my name?" Then he blessed him there.

So Jacob called the place Peniel, saying, "It is because I saw God face to face, and yet my life was spared." (Genesis 32:24-30)

Talk about a shapeshifter! Theologians still debate whether this was an angel, God in the form of a man—Christ before he was incarnate as Jesus of Nazareth—or some other manifestation of God. This encounter changed Jacob's name to Israel, but his struggles were not over yet. Israel became the father of twelve brothers. He favored one son, Joseph, who was the firstborn of Jacob's beloved Rachel. When Joseph was a teen, his jealous older brothers sold Joseph as a slave to passing traders and led his father to believe Joseph had been torn by beasts and killed.

Israel lived many years suffering under this deception, until God orchestrated another family reunion, where a positive shapeshifter would be unveiled. Joseph miraculously survived many difficulties to be raised up as second in command of Egypt, in charge of the only food supply in the region during a severe famine. When the sons of Israel were forced to find food or die, they went to Joseph, dressed and living as an Egyptian official, although they they didn't recognize him. After several episodes of testing and toying with his brothers, Joseph unmasked himself as their brother. They were afraid, but

> Joseph said to them, "Don't be afraid. Am I in the place of God? You intended to harm me, but God intended it for good to accomplish what is now being done, the saving of many lives. So then, don't be afraid. I will provide for you and your children." And he reassured them and spoke kindly to them. (Genesis 50:19-21)

Even though Joseph's brothers intended evil, God used their trickery to bring about good in the end. Jacob/Israel reaped what he had sown, but we see that God is able even to use duplicitous people who live as shapeshifters to accomplish good that they never intended or imagined. God is proven dependable even when working through shapeshifters.

God is the Author of our story as he was of Joseph's, and if we have entrusted our lives to God, we can rest assured that he can sort out the shapeshifters in our lives, even when we aren't able to protect ourselves against them initially. Jesus told a parable along these lines, saying:

> The kingdom of heaven is like a man who sowed good seed in his field. But while everyone was sleeping, his enemy came and sowed weeds among the wheat, and went away. When the wheat sprouted and formed heads, then the weeds also appeared.
>
> The owner's servants came to him and said, "Sir, didn't you sow good seed in your field? Where then did the weeds come from?"
>
> "An enemy did this," he replied.
>
> The servants asked him, "Do you want us to go and pull them up?"
>
> "No," he answered, "because while you are pulling the weeds, you may root up the wheat with them. Let both grow together until the harvest. At that time I will tell the harvesters: First collect the

weeds and tie them in bundles to be burned; then gather the wheat and bring it into my barn." (Matthew 13:24-30)

The people listening lived in an agricultural community, familiar with wheat harvests and weeds that could ruin the harvest. One common weed, also known as a tare, was an agricultural shapeshifter which grew up looking similar to wheat. When the wheat ripened, the much darker, differently shaped tares were revealed as weeds. These weeds also had a tendency to entangle their roots with the good wheat, so that if you pulled up a weed, you would also hurt the good stalks of grain.

Jesus provided the key to understand this parable:

- The one who sowed the good seed is the Son of Man (that's Jesus).
- The field is the world (not the church, but the world including the church).
- The good seed stands for the sons of the kingdom.
- The weeds are the sons of the evil one (the devil).
- The enemy who sows them is the devil.
- The harvest is the end of the age.
- The harvesters are angels.

Jesus explained:

As the weeds are pulled up and burned in the fire, so it will be at the end of the age. The Son of Man will send out his angels, and they will weed out of his kingdom everything that causes sin and all who do evil. They will throw them into the fiery furnace, where there will be weeping and gnashing of teeth. Then the righteous will shine like the sun in the kingdom of their Father. He who has ears, let him hear. (Matthew 13:40-43)

This is important for us on two counts; one is to realize that people are not what they seem on the surface. This is especially true of people

with evil intentions who want to mingle unnoticed among good society; therefore, beware.

The other point is that God will do the final sorting. We are to be cautious but trust that God will sort everyone out on Judgment Day. Hebrews 4:13 promises, "Nothing in all creation is hidden from God's sight. Everything is uncovered and laid bare before the eyes of him to whom we must give account." We can trust that nothing slips past God. God knows the true nature of the shapeshifter and each one of us will be unveiled before him some day.

AM I A SHAPESHIFTER?

In real life, people aren't all good or all evil. When we look at ourselves honestly, we realize that we often struggle back and forth, like Lando Calrissian, between being allies or enemies. The apostle Paul describes this internal struggle in Romans 7; he does the things he doesn't want to do, and doesn't do the good he really wants to do.

We also run into people with hidden agendas. They may be con artists or someone close, parents or friends who put on an act and betray our trust. You may think of religious leaders (pedophile priests come to mind, along with certain discredited televangelists) whose sanctimonious garb makes others unlikely to conceive of their evil acts or an unfaithful spouse, or a Christian business partner who rips off a trusting co-laborer. All those who put on a good front to cover evil acts are represented by the archetype of the shapeshifter.

We must beware of shapeshifters especially where God's work is going forward. That is where the enemy will want to do the most damage. Given the prevalence of shapeshifters I have come to agree with Psalm 118:8: "It is better to take refuge in the LORD than to trust in man." God's nature and intentions toward us remain unchanging. As we sing to God in the grand old hymn, "Thou changeth not! Thy compassions they fail not! As Thou hast been thou forever will be. Great is thy faithfulness!"

Malachi 3:6 reads "I the LORD do not change"; James affirms God's constant nature of goodness: "Every good and perfect gift is from above, coming down from the Father of the heavenly lights, who does not change like shifting shadows" (James 1:17).

Even though God's nature does not change, there was one monumental case where he acted as a shapeshifter for our good. Jesus lowered himself from the eternal glories of heaven where he had always existed, and took on the form of sinful humanity.

> Being in very nature God,
>> [Jesus] did not consider equality with God something to be
>> grasped,
> but made himself nothing,
>> taking the very nature of a servant,
>> being made in human likeness.
> And being found in appearance as a man,
>> he humbled himself
>> and became obedient to death—even death on a cross!
> (Philippians 2:6-8)

Jesus—God eternal—came to earth disguised as a baby, a poor peasant Jew. He took on human flesh and entered our world, where we were condemned to die for our sins. He lived a sinless life, perfect God and perfect man, and then he chose to die on the cross. Since he had never sinned, death could not hold him. He rose from the dead and gave us the opportunity to, in him, receive a pardon, receive eternal life and go free. Therefore, Paul taught,

> if anyone is in Christ, he is a new creation; the old has gone, the new has come! All this is from God, who reconciled us to himself through Christ and gave us the ministry of reconciliation: that God was reconciling the world to himself in Christ, not counting men's

sins against them. And he has committed to us the message of reconciliation. We are therefore Christ's ambassadors, as though God were making his appeal through us. We implore you on Christ's behalf: Be reconciled to God. (2 Corinthians 5:17-20)

The very next verse says, "God made him who had no sin to be sin for us, so that in him we might become the righteousness of God" (2 Corinthians 5:21). Jesus the benevolent shapeshifter makes a spiritual swap without the use of polyjuice potion. And what is to be the outcome? We certainly are not to use our freedom to do evil or to indulge our sinful nature. The apostle Peter taught us, "Live as free men, but do not use your freedom as a cover-up for evil; live as servants of God" (1 Peter 2:16). Similarly, Paul taught, "You . . . were called to be free. But do not use your freedom to indulge the sinful nature; rather, serve one another in love" (Galatians 5:13). We are to go out and tell others that they too can escape the penalty and incarceration of sin.

So, as we go forward in our battles against evil, let us beware of shapeshifters. Let's recognize that people are not always as they appear; spiritual forces often work through shapeshifters. But let us also appreciate Christ's adventure as a shapeshifter to free us from the power of sin and the penalty of death. We can trust that the Author of our story is able to handle the shapeshifters in our life's story well enough to lead us to a good ending.

Of course, with most fantasy stories the characters don't move directly from their beginnings to a good end. Before they get there they must face the ultimate battle of their quest. We will look at the theme of fighting ultimate battles in our next chapter.

10

Fighting the Ultimate Battles

"Don't be afraid of them. Remember the Lord, who is great and awesome, and fight for your brothers, your sons and your daughters, your wives and your homes."

Nehemiah 4:14

Fantastic stories lead up to a final showdown between the forces of good and evil, an ultimate battle in which justice must be upheld or restored, and either the hero or the villain will be destroyed. Every great fantasy story, and the Bible itself, leads to an ultimate battle between the forces of good and evil, between the villain and the hero. The ultimate battle does more than test the mettle of the hero team; it determines who will live, who will die, and who will rule the world (whatever world that might be).

The Christian life contains a paradox; we are assured of ultimate victory but must face life's battles. Theologically we know that Christ ultimately defeated Satan on the cross; his victory is proved by his resurrection. Those who believe the Bible are confident—having read the end of our world's story—that Satan and evil will ultimately be defeated. In the meantime, however, "we know that we are children of God, and that the whole world is under the control of the evil one" (1 John 5:19). So the battles against evil continue every day.

Usually, our battles in life are not as monumental as the ones we think of as ultimate battles, but each battle against evil does its part, and each person fighting against evil makes a difference—whether in a school yard, in our family, in our society or within the secret places of our own hearts. So, biblically, we believe that the ultimate battle will be won by God and those on his side. In the meantime, we have to occupy this world and fight back against the forces of evil wherever we face them, even when it seems we face a losing battle.

Our daily battles against evil do matter. Consider Dumbledore's words to Harry after his first showdown with Voldemort in *Harry Potter and the Sorcerer's Stone.*

> Harry asked, "Well, Voldemort's going to try other ways of coming back, isn't he? I mean, he hasn't gone has he?"
>
> "No, Harry, he has not. He is still out there somewhere, perhaps looking for another body to share . . . not being truly alive, he cannot be killed. He left Quirrell to die; he shows just as little mercy to his followers as his enemies. Nevertheless, Harry, while you may only have delayed his return to power, it will merely take someone else who is willing to fight what seems a losing battle next time— and if he is delayed again, and again, why, he may never return to power."

Even though Dumbledore could have intervened, he allowed Harry and his fellow students to learn to fight in the battle, to take their fall if necessary. Some of those on the hero team even died. However, regardless of the high price to be paid, fighting against evil is necessary because evil is aggressive. So too in our world; even though it may seem that evil is rampant, we must not give up in any of our battles against evil.

In books or movies ultimate battles arise typically toward the end, but in real life it could happen at any time. Each person must choose a side and take part.

PERILS OF APPEASEMENT

Some think they can stay out of life's battles, but evil is aggressive, and therefore appeasement and turning a blind eye to wrongdoing and evil are not good options. British Prime Minister Neville Chamberlain could attest to this reality in our world (during World War II he tried to appease Adolf Hitler and declared "peace in our time," only to ultimately watch Hitler cut a genocidal path across Europe). Cornelius Fudge, Minister of Magic in Harry Potter's wizarding world, could testify to the same. During Harry's first five years at Hogwarts, Fudge tried to maintain the status quo. He had convincing evidence that Voldemort had returned when he discovered Barty Crouch Jr. disguised as Professor Moody, but Fudge didn't want to upset people, and he didn't want to *believe* such evil had re-emerged. So he covered up the evidence. He tried to use the *Daily Prophet* to discredit Harry and Dumbledore so no one would believe their testimony. His decision to deny evil when it stared him in the face, to ignore it while appeasing the Dementors, cost Fudge his position; it also cost the wizarding community at large. Being lulled into complacency left them unprepared for the ultimate battle.

In the Chronicles of Narnia, Aslan recognizes the aggressive nature of evil and the need to destroy it when he prepares his forces before the Battle of Beruna against the forces of the White Witch. He knows the evil forces will attack, so he instructs Peter to lead the forces of good to oppose them.

In the first three *Star Wars* films, Anakin Skywalker makes the mistake of not opposing evil relentlessly. He tries to get close to Chancellor Palpatine (whom we come to recognize as the evil Darth Sidius), working with him even after Palpatine orders him to kill Dooku, which he knows to be wrong. What might have happened if Anakin opposed the chancellor outright when he called for defiance of the Jedi Code? By the end of the series, Anakin realizes that the only way to deal effectively with such evil is to stand against it with all his might, but such knowledge, coming too late, cost him his life.

In fantastic stories, and our own history, we learn that for life to be good, good must triumph over evil. But that doesn't happen without forceful action of some kind. Compromise is unwise; evil is active and will advance if left unchecked. When evil will not relent, it must be confronted and conquered—not coddled. These battles against evil may be spiritual—battles of prayer, relentless love or speaking the truth—but they must be forceful.

One of the beauties of a fantasy story is the use of monstrous creatures that are set in their nature and will not be persuaded to change. The reader is sure that a basilisk, the king of snakes, will not be made into a pet. Therefore, an ultimate battle is inevitable. In *Harry Potter and the Chamber of Secrets* the heir of Slytherin and his monstrous basilisk target mudbloods and muggleborns for death. Harry and those on his side have to find and stop them. Although most heroes would choose redemption over destruction, their duty to defeat clear evil is required to make their world safe again.

The Bible has plenty of battles, both military and spiritual. It may not be considered politically correct to focus on them in some circles, but both the Old and the New Testament show an eventual showdown between good and evil, God's people against Satan's forces. The battle between good and evil continues on this earth, therefore, and those on the side of good must continue to participate in the battles, because evil will not back down of its own volition.

ULTIMATE BATTLES ARE VIOLENT

C. S. Lewis concluded the Chronicles of Narnia with *The Last Battle,* which chronicles the final battle between those on Aslan's side—from our world, Narnia and surrounding countries—versus those who hold no allegiance to Aslan. In that battle, combatants on Aslan's side are not shy about saying they wish to kill their enemies. King Tirian of Narnia declares his enemy Tash to be a "foul fiend" and vows to prove it with his body (thus devoting himself to physical combat if necessary). He declares the Ape, who has misled people about Aslan, a "manifold traitor" and says that the Calormenes are worthy of death. He calls all true Narnians to his side and asks, "Would you wait till your new masters have killed you all one by one?"

Lewis had to deal with criticism for the realistic battle scenes he included in his children's stories, but he defended them as necessary. In his essay "On Three Ways of Writing for Children" he agreed that a story for children should not give a child "haunting, disabling, pathological fears against which ordinary courage is helpless." However, we should not "try to keep out of his mind the knowledge that he is born into a world of death, violence, wounds, adventure, heroism and cowardice, good and evil." He goes on to differentiate the complaints of his critics:

> If they mean the first [causing haunting, disabling fears] I agree with them: but not if they mean the second. The second would indeed be to give children a false impression and feed them on escapism in the bad sense. There is something ludicrous in the idea of so educating a generation which is born to the Ogpu and the atomic bomb. Since it is so likely that they will meet cruel enemies, let them at least have heard of brave knights and heroic courage. Otherwise you are making their destiny not brighter but darker. Nor do most of us find that violence and bloodshed, in a story, produce any haunting dread in the minds of children. As far as that goes, I side impenitently with the human race against the modern reformer. Let there be wicked kings and beheadings, battles and dungeons, giants and dragons, and let villains be soundly killed at the end of the book. Nothing will persuade me that this causes an ordinary child any kind or degree of fear beyond what it wants,

and needs, to feel. For, of course, it wants to be a little frightened."[1]

The Gospel of Matthew includes an enigmatic verse I quote here in two versions. It relates to a violent struggle between the kingdom of heaven and the forces of Satan/evil:

From the days of John the Baptist until now, the kingdom of heaven has been forcefully advancing, and forceful men lay hold of it. (Matthew 11:12 NIV)

And from the days of John the Baptist until now the kingdom of heaven suffereth violence, and the violent take it by force. (KJV)

The kingdom of heaven came forcefully and with power. "God anointed Jesus of Nazareth with the Holy Spirit and power, and . . . he went around doing good and healing all who were under the power of the devil, because God was with him" (Acts 10:38). Jesus was aggressively taking back territory previously controlled by the evil one. What Jesus did was good but also forceful. Jesus cleared the temple of money changers and those selling sacrificial animals and otherwise making his Father's house a den of thieves. He could have just reasoned with them, but he threw over their tables. He could have suggested that they move along, but he made a whip out of cords and drove them out. He saw their abuse of sincere worshipers for their own gain as evil and he took action against it.

Jesus went about breaking the hold of evil over the lives of people with whom he came in contact, whether in the form of disease, demon possession, or sin. As the kingdom of heaven gained ground, forceful and violent people opposed Jesus and his followers, leading to Jesus' extremely violent death and the persecution of his followers that carries on today in some parts of our world. Just as the forces of evil take powerful and violent action, those who serve the kingdom of heaven must forcefully oppose evil.

What Is at Stake?

When good and evil face off the stakes are high. These are our "ultimate battles" that must take precedence over the everyday cares of life. In *Harry Potter and the Sorcerer's Stone,* we see Harry faced with such a battle when he realizes that he has to get to the Sorcerer's Stone before the thief. Ron calls Harry mad; Hermione warns that he might be expelled. Of the three, only Harry, grasps that this is an ultimate battle.

"SO WHAT?" Harry shouted. "Don't you understand? If Snape gets hold of the Stone, Voldemort's coming back! Haven't you heard what it was like when he tried to take over? There won't be any Hogwarts to get expelled from! He'll flatten it, or turn it into a school for the Dark Arts! Losing points doesn't matter anymore, can't you see? D'you think he'll leave you and your families alone if Gryffindor wins the house cup? If I get caught before I get to the Stone, well, I'll have to go back to the Dursleys and wait for Voldemort to find me there, it's only dying a bit later than I would have, because I'm never going over to the Dark Side!"

Harry understood that the villain had to be destroyed, or at least kept from having control, if his world was to be safe, even temporarily. So too, our ultimate battles must be recognized, we must see what's at stake and get our priorities straight so that we can fight with all our might. In our fantasy stories the battles take place between X-wing fighters and starships in a galaxy far, far, away, or on battlefields with mythic creatures, or between wizards fighting with wands and curses. But these are figurative of what life's real battles are about, where they really take place and what is truly at stake. I see the ultimate battles we face in life as these:

- battles for the souls of people
- battles for the well-being of our family, friends, and loved ones
- societal battles for the preservation of freedom and goodness in civilization
- battles for justice in an unjust world

We fight for souls. Harry fought off the Dementors, who would have sucked out Dudley's soul. Even though he was not fond of Dudley, he was the only one there to do battle to save his soul. Family, friends, co-workers, neighbors—everyone in our circle of influence—these are people for whom we should care about the eternal state of their souls. We have power in prayer and should be praying for their souls to be saved. When we have opportunity we should do our very best to present the gospel of salvation and answer their questions so as to lead them to Christ. When they are hurting, we should demonstrate love that may draw them to the one who can save their souls. If we know that someone we love is not safely in Christ, we must do battle for them in prayer now, and take every opportunity to convince them of what is at stake so they are not lost.

We fight to protect our family and friends. Luke fought to rescue Han Solo and Leia from Jabba the Hutt. (My daughter points out that Princess Leia did quite a good job of fighting on her own behalf as well as helping Han and Luke too!) In our world the dangers may not be quite as ugly as Jabba, but are dangerous none the less. We must be active in protecting those we love, the relationships we hold dear. Parents cannot be lax when children are veering off into something wrong or hurtful; we can't ignore when children fall in with the wrong crowd—not if we are going to protect them. We have to be active in prayer, leadership, supervision and discipline. We can't simply trust that since we married a Christian our marriage is set for life. We must be vigilant in guarding our marital relationship by maintaining personal holiness, staying connected, praying for our spouse and our marriage, and fighting to save our marriage if it gets in trouble.[2]

There are people in your family who need you to fight the good fight to guard their souls and benefit their lives. God will show you who and how to battle on their behalf. I love the part of the book of Nehemiah where the people of Israel are trying to rebuild the wall that will keep the enemies out of Jerusalem. Each family group built and battled at the point in the wall that was adjacent to their home. Some people would serve as sentries while working on the wall—a sword in one hand and a trowel in the other. Others then could continue building under their protection. When the enemies attacked, Nehemiah said, "Don't be afraid of them. Remember the Lord, who is great and awesome, and fight for your brothers, your sons and your daughters, your wives and your homes" (Nehemiah 4:14). We need to take the same stance, building for the future while remaining on guard to protect our loved ones. And we have one of the most powerful weapons known to humanity, but not known to the evil one—at least it is not in his arsenal—the power of love.

Since love is the ultimate weapon that the enemy does not understand, we have an advantage whenever we face our battles against evil with love. As the Bible says, love never fails.

We fight to protect our society from tyranny and oppression; we fight for goodness sake. In several of the stories in the Chronicles of Narnia we see those whose power was unjustly usurped restored to their rightful position, as with Prince Rilian in *The Silver Chair* and the title character in the book *Prince Caspian.* We also see the slave trade suspended in *Voyage of the "Dawn Treader."* In *Star Wars* the rebel alliance fights the Empire to restore freedom to the galaxy. Harry Potter's ultimate battles are to protect the entire wizarding world (and our "muggle" world too) from the tyranny of evil. Such stories help us think through the need for just societies to defend themselves against evil aggression and to free others from tyranny when it is in our power to do so.

C. S. Lewis wrote in the early 1950s, shortly after the conclusion of World War II. His adventures in *The Lion, the Witch and the Wardrobe* are set during a time when children really were sent away from London because of Nazi air raids. He wrote of Jadis using the Deplorable Word to destroy her world against the backdrop of the Manhattan Project, when the newly created nuclear bomb made it possible for the first time in history to destroy all life on our planet. Lewis understood the intentions of evil on the march and the imperative to fight evil fiercely.

The original *Star Wars* trilogy (episodes four, five and six) were written in the 1970s and reflect the political climate of the times. One copy of the script makes reference to "Nixonian goons" in the margin, a reflection of the 1970s popular backlash against the scandal-ridden President Nixon. Also casting a shadow over *Star Wars* was the Viet Nam War and the ongoing Cold War between the communist Soviet Union and the United States. One might wonder how far, far away the evil Emperor was from President Reagan's reference to the Soviet Union as an "Evil Empire" in the public consciousness?

The *Harry Potter* stories, written at the turn of the twenty-first century, offer instructive parallels to a real-world "war on terror." The struggles we see in the wizarding world over whether to acknowledge that Voldemort is back or that there are Death Eaters hiding in "sleeper cells" among them is similar to the way our world is struggling with the implications of global terrorism. In *Harry Potter and the Chamber of Secrets,* those trying to destroy Hogwarts are living among them, hiding in plain sight; the children must learn not to discriminate against everyone in a certain house or blood-line while trying to protect themselves from a stealthy enemy. In our world, terrorist faces mixed in unnoticed among crowds of travelers at several American airports in 2001, sat unrecognized on a train in Madrid in 2004, rode a double-decker bus on a busy London street in 2005, even boarded a train at Kings Cross Station— ultimately killing many innocent travelers.

The Death Eaters in Harry Potter's wizarding world adore "pure blood"—full-blooded wizards—and discriminate against anyone with mixed blood ("mudbloods") and those who want to protect "muggles" (nonwizards). Some consider it significant that Harry's mentor, Albus Dumbledore, is considered particularly famous for his defeat of a dark wizard in 1945, the same year Hitler died and the Nazis were defeated.

In *Goblet of Fire,* Hagrid reassured Harry over the return of the evil wizard Voldemort. "Known it fer years, Harry. Knew he was out there bidin' his time. It had ter happen. Well now it has, an we'll just' have ter get on with it. We'll fight." Seeing Harry and his friends refuse to cower before such evil can give children courage to face the evil out there, bidin' its time among us. They don't necessarily need to join the military, they could also fight evil through public service, volunteerism and political action to uphold righteousness and justice. Hermione's Society for the Promotion of Elfish Welfare, a one-woman campaign on behalf of house-elves, is a good example of overcoming injustice with justice.

FIGHTING INJUSTICE

Ultimate battles promote justice. In *The Lion, the Witch and the Wardrobe* we see Aslan's absolute commitment to justice, even when justice required someone to die. Indeed, a Narnian prophecy foretold not only that Aslan would come but that part of his purpose for coming was to bring justice: "Wrong will be right when Aslan comes in sight." When the Deep Magic, instituted at the creation of Narnia by Aslan's Father, the Emperor Beyond the Sea, required a death sentence for Edmund's transgression, Susan whispered to Aslan, "Isn't there something you can work against it?"

> "Work against the Emperor's Magic?" said Aslan turning to her with something like a frown on his face. And nobody ever made that suggestion to him again.

We realize by Aslan's reaction that justice must be satisfied regardless the cost. However, when Aslan satisfied justice by offering himself to die as a substitute for Edmund, his death caused death itself to work backward. So justice and life triumphed together.

This combination of self-sacrifice and bringing about justice is described in the book of Romans where the apostle Paul explains of Jesus' death:

> God presented him as a sacrifice of atonement, through faith in his blood. He did this to demonstrate his justice, because in his forbearance he had left the sins committed beforehand unpunished. He did it to demonstrate his justice at the present time, so as to be just and the one who justifies those who have faith in Jesus. (Romans 3:25-26)

The entire story of *Harry Potter and the Prisoner of Azkaban* revolves around righting the wrongful imprisonment of Sirius Black. Working on the side of good, fighting evil, Black was nonetheless wrongly accused of murdering thirteen people. He spent many years in Azkaban prison, for this crime he did not commit, before finally escaping to confront the person who actually committed the crimes. A similar battle took place as Harry and friends tried to save Buckbeak, a Hippogriff (part horse, part bird). Through a sham trial Buckbeak was condemned to be executed by a member of the Ministry of Magic who was secretly a Death Eater. In both cases, Harry and Hermione desperately appealed to Dumbledore, who helped them find Sirius and encouraged them, "If all goes well, you will be able to save more than one innocent life tonight."

THE ULTIMATE WEAPON IN ULTIMATE BATTLES

The Bible has much to say about fighting injustice. The book of Job says that God "saves the needy from the sword in their mouth; he saves them from the clutches of the powerful. So the poor have hope, and injustice shuts its mouth" (Job 5:15-16).

Saving the poor and oppressed from injustice is not just God's job; it's been assigned to God's people. The prophet Micah proclaimed,

> He has showed you, O man, what is good.

And what does the LORD require of you?
To act justly and to love mercy
 and to walk humbly with your God. (Micah 6:8)

The Bible beautifully and practically describes a powerful weapon that befuddles enemies and through which good overcomes evil. The ultimate weapon is love.

Love is patient, love is kind. It does not envy, it does not boast, it is not proud. It is not rude, it is not self-seeking, it is not easily angered, it keeps no record of wrongs. Love does not delight in evil but rejoices with the truth. It always protects, always trusts, always hopes, always perseveres. Love never fails. (1 Corinthians 13:4-8)

The power of love can save a troubled marriage, can turn lost souls to Christ, convincing them that they can break free from the bondage of sin to live a new life. Love is supernatural, and God has an endless supply that he is willing to channel through our lives if we are willing to distribute it. And love never delights in evil!

Love is also Harry Potter's secret weapon. It saves him at the end of book five in *Harry Potter and the Order of the Phoenix,* although he seems to underestimate its worth. Dumbledore explains to Harry:

"You have a power that Voldemort never had. You can—"

"I know!" said Harry impatiently. "I can love!" It was only with difficulty that he stopped himself adding, "Big deal!"

"Yes, Harry, you can love," said Dumbledore, who looked as thought he knew perfectly well what Harry had just refrained from saying. "Which, given everything that has happened to you, is a great and remarkable thing."

As we consider our personal lives, let us make sure that we give the ultimate battles of life the priority attention they deserve, seeking to save souls, protect our family, preserve good in society and fight injustice. In so doing we will be contributing to the victory of good over evil in our world.

There is one other kind of ultimate battle so important it deserves its own chapter: combating the shadow of our own dark nature. We take that up in our next chapter.

11

Combating the Shadow of Our Own Dark Nature

"Voldemort put a bit of himself in *me?*" Harry said, thunderstruck.

Harry Potter and the Chamber of Secrets

There is one other kind of "ultimate battle" we see in all our fantasy stories. It is perhaps the most profound because it is one each person must face alone.

In *Star Wars: The Empire Strikes Back* Yoda sends Luke out alone, past a snake in a tree and into the misty darkness of a cave. Yoda tells Luke not to take his weapons with him, apparently understanding that the battle will not be external. But Luke takes his light saber anyway and comes upon the mystic image of his nemesis, Darth Vader. They fight, and Luke decapitates the image of Darth Vader, but suddenly his own face is revealed behind the villain's mask.

Luke is shaken by his encounter in the cave, but he leaves determined never to go over to the dark side. Even so, Yoda refers to this battle as a failure. Ever wonder why? The best I can conclude is that it has more to do with Luke's inner battle with evil than with his ongoing conflict with Darth Vader.

We all, like Luke, must face the shadow of our own dark nature at some time. This is perhaps the most important battle for anyone. Those who study the mythic archetypes of classic stories sometimes call the villain the shadow, representing a dark replica of what the hero could become. The hero discovers in him- or herself something of the villain's nature. According to *The Writer's Journey*, the "shadow represents the energy of the dark side . . . suppressed monsters of our inner world. Shadows can be all the things we don't like about ourselves, all the dark secrets we can't admit, even to ourselves, the qualities we have renounced and tried to root out, but still lurk within."[1] Biblically speaking, this would be called our sin nature or "the flesh."

SINS OF THE FATHERS, SHADOWS OF THE SONS

The conflict between Luke Skywalker and the image of Darth Vader in the cave on Dagoba also illustrates another biblical principle: the sins of the fathers overshadowing the lives of their children. Something of the sin nature of Anakin Skywalker, who has become Darth Vader, is resident in his son, Luke—even when Luke is not aware of their familial connection.

Our resemblance to other human beings has something to do with our universal inclination to sin. We inherited a nature with potential for good but a propensity for evil. Our susceptibility to and inclination toward evil came down to us though our family line going all the way back to the fall of humanity. Might we harbor a deeply hidden fear that we are more like the villain than we'd like to admit—especially when we are alone in the dark? The apostle Paul describes it like this:

> I do not understand what I do. For what I want to do I do not do, but what I hate I do. And if I do what I do not want to do, I agree that the law is good. As it is, it is no longer I myself who do it, but it is sin living in me. I know that nothing good lives in me, that is,

in my sinful nature. For I have the desire to do what is good, but I cannot carry it out. For what I do is not the good I want to do; no, the evil I do not want to do—this I keep on doing. Now if I do what I do not want to do, it is no longer I who do it, but it is sin living in me that does it. (Romans 7:15-20)

Rowling explores this idea of struggling with our inner likeness to the evil one through Harry's encounter with Tom Riddle (the disguised Voldemort) in the *Chamber of Secrets*. Riddle points out remarkable similarities between them, which causes Harry to worry. He confides in Dumbledore.

"Riddle said I'm like him. Strange likenesses, he said . . ."

"Did he, now?" said Dumbledore, looking thoughtfully at Harry from under his thick silver eyebrows. "And what do you think, Harry?"

"I don't think I'm like him!" said Harry, more loudly than he'd intended. "I mean, I'm—I'm in *Gryffindor,* I'm . . ."

But he fell silent, a lurking doubt resurfacing in his mind.

"Professor," he started again after a moment. "The Sorting Hat told me I'd—I'd have done well in Slytherin. Everyone thought *I* was Slytherin's heir for a while . . . because I can speak Parseltongue. . . ."

"You can speak Parseltongue, Harry," said Dumbledore calmly, "because Lord Voldemort—who *is* the last remaining ancestor of Salazar Slytherin—can speak Parseltongue. Unless I'm much mistaken, he transferred some of his own powers to you the night he gave you that scar. Not something he intended to do. I'm sure. . . ."

"Voldemort put a bit of himself in *me*?" Harry said, thunderstruck.

"It certainly seems so. . . . Listen to me Harry. You happen to have many qualities Salazar Slytherin prized in his hand-picked students. His own very rare gift, Parseltongue—resourcefulness—determination—a certain disregard for rules," he added, his mustache quivering again. "Yet the Sorting Hat placed you in Gryffindor. You know why that was. Think."

"It only put me in Gryffindor," said Harry in a defeated voice, "because I asked not to go in Slytherin . . ."

"*Exactly*," said Dumbledore, beaming once more. "Which makes you *very different* from Tom Riddle. It is our choices, Harry, that show what we truly are, far more than our abilities."

Like Harry, we inherit an internal struggle with sin, but we can make choices leading us away from evil. As Jesus taught us, we can pray, "Lead us not into temptation, but deliver us from evil." Would this be in the Lord's Prayer if it weren't important to address? This wrestling with sin goes on within each of us and is won not by force of will or an outward weapon, but it is settled for us as it was for Harry by *whose house we are in*.

Paul concluded Romans 7 with this declaration:

What a wretched man I am! Who will rescue me from this body of death? Thanks be to God—through Jesus Christ our Lord! . . . Therefore, there is now no condemnation for those who are *in Christ Jesus*. (Romans 7:24—8:1)

Through the power of his divine nature, Jesus can overcome our self-doubt and self-condemnation and give us supernatural power to win our inner struggles against sin.

A WAY OF ESCAPE FROM OUR DARK NATURE

There may come a point in our struggle with sin where it seems that sin has overpowered us, that we have gone too far down the dark path to resist evil. But God's word declares that there is always a way of escape from sin.

No temptation has seized you except what is common to man. And God is faithful; he will not let you be tempted beyond what you can bear. But when you are tempted, he will also provide a way out so that you can stand up under it. (1 Corinthians 10:13)

In *The Voyage of the "Dawn Treader,"* Eustace sneaks off away from the others on the *Dawn Treader* while they are repairing the ship after the sea serpent attack. He wanders over the peaks of the mountains and comes to a valley where he observes a dragon near a pool. He is afraid and disgusted by the dragon, but after observing that it seems to be ill or even dead, he makes his way into its cave. There he finds treasures, mounds of gold, precious stones, crowns and coins. He takes a gold and diamond bracelet from the pile and places it on his arm, and falls asleep. He awakens with the horrified sense that there is a dragon in the cave with him, but the dragon turns out to be him; the bracelet he coveted and took is now cutting into his dragonish flesh.

Eustace has to find a way to be released from his dragon's flesh before he is permanently cut off from his mates and left to live and die as a dragon. He attempts to scratch his dragonish flesh off, and some scales do fall off, but the dragon's nature goes to the core of his being. He eventually gives up on this pointless and painful self-effort. That's when Aslan comes. Aslan immerses Eustace in the cleansing pool but then goes on to cut him deeply. Although this hurt, once is not enough; Aslan had to repeat the procedure several times before Eustace emerged from the pool a new boy.

The only way to win the battle with the sin nature is for it to die. Like a snakeskin, Eustace sheds his dragonskin until it lies lifeless on the side of the pool. So too with our battle with the "dark side" of our nature. It's not a matter of self-improvement or scraping off a few isolated sin cells. It requires putting the old nature to death, and experiencing the power of Christ's resurrected life within us.

This is what Paul refers to in his letter to Galatians: "I have been crucified with Christ and I no longer live, but Christ lives in me. The life I live in the body, I live by faith in the Son of God, who loved me and gave himself for me" (Galatians 2:20). This is the same Paul who wrote about his inner struggle with sin in Romans 7. How are we set free from the body of this death? Through Christ Jesus! We are immersed in him, where we die to our old sin nature and are raised to new life in Christ. Paul explains this further:

> Don't you know that all of us who were baptized into Christ Jesus were baptized into his death? We were therefore buried with him through baptism into death in order that, just as Christ was raised from the dead through the glory of the Father, we too may live a new life. (Romans 6:3-4)

On a practical note, we are instructed to

> count yourselves dead to sin but alive to God in Christ Jesus. Therefore do not let sin reign in your mortal body so that you obey its evil desires. Do not offer the parts of your body to sin, as instruments of wickedness, but rather offer yourselves to God, as those who have been brought from death to life; and offer the parts of your body to him as instruments of righteousness. (Romans 6:11-13)

It may help to remember that this very difficult, very personal battle is part of every great hero's journey. Eustace wasn't restored immediately, but when he came out of the water the cure had begun. This is a lovely picture of the kind of process we must go through when we combat our sin nature.

CHOICES

Daily we make a choice: we will yield ourselves to sin and obey its evil desires, or we will submit the parts of our body—including our mind— to God as instruments of righteousness. We choose whether to yield our mortal bodies to good or evil. We need to practice this in little matters so that we can be better able to win our combat with the shadow of our own dark nature.

This yielding includes tending to our inner lives and emotions. Yoda stressed that Luke's emotions: anger, resentment, aggression, fear and the like could make him susceptible to the dark side of the force. Likewise, we would do well to attend to dark feelings; those mentioned by Yoda and also jealousy, envy, deceit, wrath, malice, and so on. Left unchecked these can leave us susceptible to losing the battle against our dark nature. This is affirmed by the Bible:

> Therefore each of you must put off falsehood and speak truthfully to his neighbor, for we are all members of one body. "In your anger do not sin": Do not let the sun go down while you are still angry, and do not give the devil a foothold. . . . And do not grieve the Holy Spirit of God, with whom you were sealed for the day of redemption. Get rid of all bitterness, rage and anger, brawling and slander, along with every form of malice. (Ephesians 4:25-31)

If we know there is something dark stirring within us, though it may seem small at the moment, we should get rid of it while it is still small. If it causes us to put on a false front or deceive those closest to us that is cause for alarm. If we are harboring anger that we hold on to over the course of days, we endanger ourselves. Any time we have to lie to ourselves and others to cover for something we are doing or thinking, any time our anger festers, we are carving out a niche the devil can use to climb into our lives.

An interesting lesson about this comes to us in the story of Cain and Abel, sons of Adam and Eve. Cain was a farmer; Abel raised livestock. God looked on Abel's blood sacrifice with more favor than he did Cain's grain offering.

So Cain was very angry, and his face was downcast.

Then the LORD said to Cain, "Why are you angry? Why is your face downcast? If you do what is right, will you not be accepted? But if you do not do what is right, sin is crouching at your door; it desires to have you, but you must master it." (Genesis 4:5-7)

At this point, God gave Cain a clear revelation of the problem: he had offered an unacceptable sacrifice. He still had a choice between right and wrong, according to God. Instead of correcting the problem, however, Cain got angry. That was the point at which sin was crouching at his door. When sin is crouching at the door, there is no time to dawdle. We must quickly take action to choose that which is right over that which our passions dictate. Cain wasn't in combat with his brother; Cain was in combat with sin and the shadow of his own dark nature. He chose not to obey God. Instead he nursed his anger and soon thereafter murdered his brother. When we choose not to deal forcefully with sin while it is still crouching at the door, be assured, it will pounce and we will pay a heavy price, as will our family and those close to us.

DEVIL'S SNARE DELIVERED GIFT-WRAPPED

Sometimes, our sin nature sneaks up on us, looking like something we can simply enjoy. In *Harry Potter and the Sorcerer's Stone,* Harry, Ron and Hermione are introduced to the Devil's Snare, a plant that is very pretty to look at but fullgrown becomes dangerous, even life-threatening. That was the intention of whoever sent the potted Devil's Snare to Mr. Bode as a Christmas gift in *Harry Potter and the Order of the Phoenix;* the plant first offered him comfort but strangled him as soon as it was big enough.

We can learn something from Rowling's depiction of the Devil's Snare: no matter how pretty it looks at first or if it is offered you as a gift, don't keep the Devil's Snare as a houseplant! As it was with Mr. Bode, so it was with Cain: neither dealt with a growing problem while they could still put an end to it. Similarly we need to deal with sin when it first enters our thoughts, before it infects our behavior. There is a connection between thinking about how to gratify the desires of the sinful nature and our eventual behavior. Romans 13:13-14 says,

> Let us behave decently, as in the daytime, not in orgies and drunkenness, not in sexual immorality and debauchery, not in dissension and jealousy. Rather, clothe yourselves with the Lord Jesus Christ, and do not think about how to gratify the desires of the sinful nature.

Whether looking at pornography or simply fantasizing about a decadent dessert, we take the first step toward behaving indecently and sinfully when we give our minds over to our sinful weakness. If you've already given the Devil's Snare a foothold, however, take heart: it is defeated by warmth and light. The Bible counsels us to bring our inner struggles into God's light and truth in prayer with someone we trust: "Therefore confess your sins to each other and pray for each other so that you may be healed. The prayer of a righteous man is powerful and effective" (James 5:16).

We need friends on our hero team who will not recoil at our inner struggles with sin but who will pray with us earnestly. The warmth of loving supportive prayer from our hero team, along with the light of God's truth and our truthful confession of the dark shadow within us, can help turn our battle against our own "Devil's Snare" into a victory. We can escape the shadow of our dark nature and be redeemed by Christ to live a new life.

Our heroes in fantasy stories must face these same daunting challenges from without and within. They must also face death—as must we all. Facing death is the subject our next chapter.

12

Facing Death, the Final Enemy

"Death, my dears" . . .

"Yes," said Professor Trelawney, nodding impres-
sively, "it comes ever closer, it circles overhead like a
vulture, ever lower . . . ever lower over the castle."

Harry Potter and the Goblet of Fire

A young boy attending his first funeral made his way to the casket at the
end of the service. He asked the man standing nearby, "Um . . . do you
know how long it will be before she disappears?"

I had to chuckle. The only understanding the boy had of death had
come from *Star Wars,* where Obi-Wan Kenobi and Yoda disappear
shortly after their deaths. He wanted to witness the grand event!

Great fantasy stories help their readers, hearers or viewers confront
and deal with the ultimate issue of death. *The Lion, the Witch and the
Wardrobe* presents the death of the lead character, Aslan. *Star Wars* shows
several lead characters passing through death's boundary, still able to encourage the living. Have you ever noticed how many fantasy stories and
fairy tales begin with the death of a parent? In *Star Wars,* Anakin Skywalker is troubled by his premonition of his mother's death and his in-
ability to keep her from dying. Luke and Leia grow up not knowing their
parents; their mother dies shortly after their birth, and their father has

"lost his life" to the dark side of the Force. Harry Potter's parents are murdered when he is an infant, and much later his godfather—the closest thing to a parent he's ever known—is murdered right in front of him. In *The Magician's Nephew,* Digory enters Narnia at its creation as his mother lay dying in our world. Digory's unexpected trip into Narnia presents him with a terrible temptation and wonderful opportunity: he is advised by Jadis to take some of the fruit from the Tree of Protection to his mother, saying it will heal her. To do so would be to disobey Aslan, however, and Digory resists the temptation, enduring the painful expectation that his mother will soon die.

At the end of *The Magician's Nephew* Digory asks Aslan to cure his dying mother. Aslan responds by weeping with him; Digory gets the sense that the Lion is sorrier about his mother's illness than he is.

> "My son, my son," said Aslan. "I know. Grief is great. Only you and I in this land know that yet. Let us be good to one another."

This reminds me of a story of Jesus weeping at the grave of a friend. Jesus knew that his friend Lazarus was going to die even before he did (although Jesus called it falling asleep), and could have healed him as he had healed many others. But Jesus had a greater plan for Lazarus than just a healing. He planned to bring Lazarus back to life. Lazarus's resurrection would be a living object lesson for Jesus' sermon: "I am the Resurrection and the Life" (John 11).

Even though Jesus knew his friend's death was about to be reversed, he wept at his tomb. What was he weeping about, really? Was it the sorrow and confusion experienced by Lazarus's sisters? Was it simply the sorrow of death itself? After all, Jesus was fully human and experienced human emotions. Whatever the reason, just as Digory was comforted by Aslan's tears, I am comforted by Jesus' tears at the graveside of his friend.

Jesus knew that when he died his followers would be consumed by grief and sorrow. Jesus offered them comfort saying, "I tell you the truth, you will weep and mourn while the world rejoices. You will grieve, but your grief will turn to joy" (John 16:20). The truth was, Jesus would defeat death and soon enough joy would replace their grief.

The Bible acknowledges the emotions that attend death: grief, even anger. Indeed, anger over death is a reasonable reaction. Death is our enemy, a fate that God did not intend for us. Death came into human experience as an attack from our enemy the devil.

In *Harry Potter and the Order of the Phoenix* Dumbledore allows Harry to vent over the death of Sirius Black by shouting and breaking things in Dumbledore's office. In *Harry Potter and the Half-Blood Prince* Hagrid grieves the death of the spider Aragog. Harry and Professor Slughorn comfort him at the grave. At the end of that book one of the series' most beloved characters dies, shocking not only the characters but the readers. I found myself angry when I read it, hoping for a resurrection in the final volume.

We should be angry about death. Death is a consequence of sin, a curse God wants to protect us from. Death is our enemy, and it is the last enemy God will destroy (1 Corinthians 15:26).

SEEKING TO COMMUNICATE ACROSS DEATH'S BOUNDARY

When Sirius Black dies Harry Potter wants to communicate with him. He doesn't consult the psychic Madam Trelawney, having concluded that she is something of a fraud, but he does try to contact Sirius using a two-way mirror Sirius gave him and, when that doesn't work, he fervently hopes Sirius will come back as a ghost.

Ghosts are prevalent in *Harry Potter.* Moaning Myrtle, the house ghosts for the four Hogwarts houses, even Professor Binns are all ghosts—sad characters who cannot eat or enjoy many of the pleasures of life. The house ghost Nearly Headless Nick persuades Harry that Sirius won't come back as a ghost but will have "gone on."

"What d'you mean, 'gone on?'" said Harry quickly. "Gone on where? Listen—what happens when you die, anyway? Where do you go? Why doesn't everyone come back? Why isn't this place full of ghosts?"

"I cannot answer," said Nick.

"You're dead, aren't you" said Harry exasperatedly. "Who can answer better than you?"

"I was afraid of death," said Nick. "I chose to remain behind. I sometimes wonder whether I oughtn't to have . . . I know nothing of the secrets of death, Harry, for I chose my feeble imitation of life instead. I believe learned wizards study the matter in the Department of Mysteries. . . . Wizards can leave an imprint of themselves upon earth, to walk palely where their living selves once trod," said Nick miserably. "But very few wizards choose that path."

In *The Silver Chair,* Eustace has just come from King Caspian's funeral in Narnia when he encounters the resurrected Caspian in Aslan's country.

"Look Here! I say," he stammered. "It's all very well. But aren't you—I mean didn't you –?"

"Oh, don't be such an ass," said Caspian.

"But," said Eustace, looking at Aslan. "Hasn't he—er—died?"

"Yes," said the Lion in a very quiet voice, almost (Jill thought) as if he were laughing. "He has died. Most people have, you know. Even I have. There are very few who haven't."

"Oh," said Caspian. "I see what's bothering you. You think I'm a ghost or some nonsense. But don't you see? I would be that if I appeared in Narnia now: because I don't belong there any more. But one can't be a ghost in one's own country. I might be a ghost if I got into your world. I don't know."

What are we to make of ghost stories? What does the Bible have to say about them? Saul, a deeply flawed king in the Old Testament, disguised himself and called on a medium to consult the spirit of the dead prophet Samuel, a violation of the law of Israel:

> Saul swore to her by the LORD, "As surely as the LORD lives, you will not be punished for this."
>
> Then the woman asked, "Whom shall I bring up for you?"
>
> "Bring up Samuel," he said.
>
> When the woman saw Samuel, she cried out at the top of her voice and said to Saul, "Why have you deceived me? You are Saul!"
>
> The king said to her, "Don't be afraid. What do you see?"
>
> The woman said, "I see a spirit coming up out of the ground."
>
> "What does he look like?" he asked.
>
> "An old man wearing a robe is coming up," she said.
>
> Then Saul knew it was Samuel. (1 Samuel 28:10-14)

Jesus' disciples believed in ghosts and thought Jesus was a ghost when they saw him walking on the water. After his resurrection, Jesus was careful to prove to his followers that he was not a ghost: he told them, "Look at my hands and my feet. It is I myself! Touch me and see; a ghost does not have flesh and bones, as you see I have" (Luke 24:39). He even ate with them to prove he was in a physical (though supernatural) body.

Beyond these examples, the Bible says little on the subject of ghosts. We're assured that we will see our loved ones again but rather than experience them coming to us, we're told that we will go to them. We are commanded not to seek to communicate with the dead through a medium, séances or other forms of the occult. The subject of ghosts, the Bible advises us, is best left in the Department of Mysteries.

I WONDER . . .

People wonder about death. Fantasy stories help us raise the right questions about death, but we need the revelation of God to give us definitive answers.

Good characters may wonder, but are not generally consumed by fear of death. In *The Horse and His Boy,* Shasta is forced to spend a night alone in the tombs, a place of death. Frightened by the roar of a lion, he thinks he will be killed by it and wonders if it will hurt and what happens to people after they're dead. In *The Magician's Nephew* the cabby, Digory, Polly, Jadis and Uncle Andrew enter Narnia at the dawn of creation and think they might be dead. The cabby tries to cheer them up by saying that worse things happen; they need not fear if they have led a decent life. Then the cabby leads the group in a hymn of thanksgiving.

One outstanding characteristic of most heroes is courage in the face of death. Our heroes find some way to overcome their fears. In *Star Wars: A New Hope* Obi-Wan Kenobi has learned enough to know death is not the end; the Force goes on. Likewise, in *Return of the Jedi* Yoda looks forward to resting in death as his twilight approaches. Both Jedis face their death with courage and calmness. In *Harry Potter and the Sorcerer's Stone* Nicolas Flamel and his wife weigh the costs and decide that they should destroy the Sorcerer's Stone, giving up their source of the Elixir of Life, rather than risk it falling in the hands of someone wicked. As Dumbledore explains to Harry, "To one as young as you, I'm sure it seems incredible, but to Nicolas and Perenelle, [facing death] really is like going to bed after a very, *very* long day. After all, to the well-organized mind, death is but the next great adventure."

Narnia too shows us characters who face death courageously. In *Prince Caspian,* Aslan and company come upon an old woman who is about to die (Caspian's nurse, who first told him the stories of Aslan and old Narnia). She faces "the long journey" of death completely unafraid because of her relationship with Aslan. Aslan instead heals her, and she follows him on his romp and is reunited with Prince Caspian. In *The Silver Chair,* Prince Rilian's shield changes to bright silver when he is freed from an enchantment. An image of the Lion appears on the shield, which he takes this to mean that, whether they live or die, Aslan will be their good lord. Anticipating that they may soon be parted by death, Rilian has everyone shake hands and courageously says, "Let us descend into the City and take the adventure that is sent us."

Villains, by contrast, typically suffer from the fear of death. The fear of death turns Anakin Skywalker to the dark side in *Star Wars:* he suffers from a premonition of his mother's death, and when he is unable to save her life, he becomes overwhelmed with fear and premonitions that his wife Padmé will die in childbirth. Darth Sidius uses this fear of death to lure Anakin, promising that the dark side of the Force offers power over death. Similarly, Harry Potter's enemy Voldemort is consumed with trying to cheat death because he fears it.

THE CURSE OF DEATH AND A POWERFUL COUNTER-CURSE

It's little wonder that the curse of death is a major theme in fantasy stories. We humans realize that everyone must face the curse of death. The Bible offers a thorough explanation of the curse of death and the powerful counter-curse provided, but even those who have only read fantasy stories would get the idea that the remedy for the curse of death comes through a willing self-sacrifice. In *Star Wars*, Obi-Wan Kenobi and ultimately Anakin Skywalker both die in order that Luke may live. Tom Riddle, the disguised Voldemort in *Harry Potter and the Chamber of Secrets,* asks why he can't kill Harry.

> "No one knows why you lost your powers when you attacked me," said Harry abruptly. "I don't know myself. But I know why you couldn't *kill* me. Because my mother died to save me. My common *Muggle-born* mother," he added shaking with suppressed rage.

Even Voldemort had to admit that Harry's mother's sacrifice was a powerful counter-charm.

Aslan, in *The Lion, the Witch and the Wardrobe,* recognizes the White Witch's "right to a kill" because of Edmund's treachery. He knows that someone must pay the penalty of death; this was written into Narnian law by Aslan's father, the Emperor Beyond the Sea, before the world began. But Aslan allows himself to be slaughtered on the Stone Table in Edmund's place. Seeing Aslan die in such a humiliating way surrounded by his enemies is terrible, but the rest of the story reveals that he is motivated by love. His death provides the "powerful counter-curse" that invokes Deeper Magic that the witch does not know. His self-sacrificial death causes death itself to start working backward.

In each of these cases someone *chooses* to die in the place of another and as a result provides life for others, even for their whole world or galaxy. All of this correlates to the Bible's assertion that the law must be satisfied with a blood sacrifice. Jesus came into a human body—subject to death—so he could face death for us and lead us courageously past it into eternal life. The blood of Jesus (one who had never sinned) willingly given for the sins of the world, broke the curse of death. The book of Hebrews explains,

> Since the children have flesh and blood, he too shared in their humanity so that by his death he might destroy him who holds the power of death—that is, the devil—and free those who all their lives were held in slavery by their fear of death. (Hebrews 2:14-15)

Knowing this gives believers courage in the face of death. We can live like heroes, unhindered by the fear that can lead others to the dark side.

LIFE AFTER DEATH

All our stories are replete with examples and encouragement that there is some kind of life after death. In *Star Wars: A New Hope,* Obi-Wan Kenobi dies and his body disappears, but he reappears in spirit form. After their deaths, Yoda and Anakin appear with Obi-Wan to comfort Luke and reassure him. In Narnia, King Tirian and his companions die and pass through golden gates into a walled garden where the Tree of Protection stands. There they are welcomed by Reepicheep, King Peter, King Edmund, Queen Lucy, King Caspian, and all the heroes of Narnia throughout history, including Tirian's own father who appears as he was when Tirian was a boy.

In *Harry Potter and the Goblet of Fire* Harry's wand wins a duel against its brother wand used by Voldemort. With that, Priori Incantatum takes place, and shadows of those killed by Voldemort's wand reappear. The apparitions briefly communicate with Harry, indicating that those who died still exist in some living form. In *Order of the Phoenix,* Harry and friends come upon the veil on the dais in the Death Chamber in the Department of Mysteries. Harry and Luna hear voices behind the veil. Later Luna reminds Harry of this to console him that Sirius is still "alive" somewhere and to assure him that they will surely see them again.

The Bible says much about life after death that is reassuring for those who trust in Jesus Christ. We are promised by Jesus himself:

> In my Father's house are many rooms; if it were not so, I would have told you. I am going there to prepare a place for you. And if I go and prepare a place for you, I will come back and take you to be with me that you also may be where I am. (John 14:2-3)

The Book of Revelation says, "He who has an ear, let him hear what the Spirit says to the churches. To him who overcomes, I will give the right to eat from the tree of life, which is in the paradise of God" (Revelation 2:7). So we can have a hopeful expectation that there is life after death and that there we will experience the fulfillment of God's original intention in the Garden of Eden.

THE SEARCH FOR IMMORTALITY

The search for immortality is a huge subject in most fantasy stories. In the Chronicles of Narnia, Jadis has immortality on her mind when she scales the wall to the garden—which is forbidden—and steals and eats some of the fruit. She tempts Digory to eat the fruit, saying that by eating it they will not grow old and die. Digory isn't so keen about living on and on, watching everyone he loves die. He says he'd rather live an ordinary time, "die and go to Heaven." As he leaves, she cries after him, telling him to think of her when he is old and dying, to remember then how he threw away the chance of having endless youth. As it turned out, this was false. Readers later learn that in Aslan's country youth is restored after death. But what did the Witch know?

In *Harry Potter and the Sorcerer's Stone,* the quest for the Sorcerer's Stone is—in part—a quest for immortality. To escape death Voldemort is willing to do something he knows will give him a cursed existence. He drinks unicorn blood and commits murders in order to make horcruxes as a safeguard against death. His evil schemes in his quest for immortality do not bode well for him.

Jesus acknowledged the desire for immortality but gave his followers a warning:

> For whoever wants to save his life will lose it, but whoever loses his life for me will find it. What good will it be for a man if he gains the whole world, yet forfeits his soul? Or what can a man give in exchange for his soul? (Matthew 16:25-26)

We are not to be like Voldemort or Jadis, who turned to the dark side in their quest for immortality. God made us to live forever, but humanity took a detour into sin and death. The Bible is a long saga of God's plans to remedy the curse of death and make a way for us to live happily ever after. The Bible has much comfort to offer regarding our quest for immortality, but God's way is through Jesus Christ, who defeated death and proved it through his resurrection and ascension. The Gospel of John declares: "For God so loved the world that he gave his one and only Son, that whoever believes in him shall not perish but have *eternal life*. For God did not send his Son into the world to condemn the world, but to save the world through him" (John 3:16-17).

So God is on a quest to bring those he created and whom he loves into eternal life. The whole Bible is related to our quest for immortality: in the garden of Eden, at the cross, at the empty tomb, and in the final chapter, where we see people finally enjoying the Tree of Life. But immortal happiness can't be stolen or gotten by disobedience. The Bible says every person is destined to pass through death and face judgment:

> Just as man is destined to die once, and after that to face judgment, so Christ was sacrificed once to take away the sins of many people; and he will appear a second time, not to bear sin, but to bring salvation to those who are waiting for him. (Hebrews 9:27-28)

A GOOD DEATH

One common theme in fantasy stories is the idea of a "good death." In *The Last Battle* the last king of Narnia and Jewel, the unicorn, know it is their last night alive. They settle accounts, although there is little to settle, because they have been good to each other. King Tirian declares that if Aslan had given him a choice he would choose no other life than the one he has led, and no other death than the one they are about to go to. It turns out that King Tirian's faith is well-founded. When they are thrown to their deaths in the stable, King Tirian is amazed to realize "that the Stable seen from within and the Stable seen from without are two different places." To this Queen Lucy replies that "in our world too, a Stable once had something inside it that was bigger than our whole world." By the end of *The Last Battle* the friends of Aslan enter into eternal life in Aslan's country.

The Last Battle also addresses the death of a world, Narnia. When Lucy cries over all that lay "dead and frozen" behind the door to Narnia Aslan has shut, Jill comforts her, saying that she too hoped Narnia might go on forever. However, as they follow Aslan "further in and further up" they discover that the real Narnia, and the real England, are contained in their new world. Their previous experiences were but poor imitations of the real life that goes on forever in Aslan's country.

The Bible tells us that our world too will be destroyed one day:

> The day of the Lord will come like a thief. The heavens will disappear with a roar; the elements will be destroyed by fire, and the earth and everything in it will be laid bare.
>
> Since everything will be destroyed in this way, what kind of people ought you to be? You ought to live holy and godly lives as you look forward to the day of God and speed its coming. That day will bring about the destruction of the heavens by fire, and the elements will melt in the heat. But in keeping with his promise we are looking forward to a new heaven and a new earth, the home of righteousness.
>
> So then, dear friends, since you are looking forward to this, make every effort to be found spotless, blameless and at peace with him. (2 Peter 3:10-14)

Those who are "friends of Jesus" can look forward to a new world where only the good remains. Yes, we still grieve and feel sorrow when we are separated from a loved one who dies, but we do not grieve as those who have no hope. We can have courage and comfort in the face of death because we are assured that death is only a transition to eternal life.

Having faced death, let us move on to explore the themes of grand rescues, resurrections, and redemption.

13

Grand Rescues, Resurrection and Redemption

"Oh, Aslan!" cried both children, staring up at him, almost as much frightened as they were glad.

"Aren't you dead, then, dear Aslan?" said Lucy.

"Not now," said Aslan.

The Lion, the Witch and the Wardrobe

"I am the resurrection and the life. He who believes in me will live, even though he dies; and whoever lives and believes in me will never die. Do you believe this?"

Jesus (John 11:25-26)

No fantasy story is complete without grand rescues, resurrection and themes of redemption. These not only make for excitement but also give the hero team a chance to sacrifice themselves to save one another and see good triumph over evil.

GRAND RESCUES

All of our fantasy stories have many examples of grand rescues. In *The*

Lion, the Witch and the Wardrobe, the dwarf suggests that the White Witch keep Edmund, her rightful prey, for bargaining with Aslan, but she knows that those on the side of good will come to rescue him. So she has him tied to a tree trunk and sharpens her knife. Aslan sends his forces and rescues Edmund in the nick of time. In The Silver Chair Eustace, Jill and Puddleglum the Marshwiggle are sent to rescue Prince Rilian from the underworld and the enchantment that holds him there. Along the way they face hungry giants and an army of mud-people, and defeat an evil enchantress. Their rescue is made possible by following the signs Aslan gives them and obeying his instructions. In The Last Battle those on Aslan's side rescue Jewel the Unicorn and Puzzle the donkey. Even though Puzzle assisted Aslan's enemies, his life is spared and he enters Aslan's country.

In Star Wars: A New Hope Obi-Wan Kenobi, Luke Skywalker and Han Solo team up to rescue Princess Leia from Darth Vader. R2-D2 and C-3PO rescue Leia, Luke and Han from a trash compactor. In The Empire Strikes Back Luke chooses to fall—supposedly to his death—rather than turn to the dark side. Leia senses he is in trouble and persuades Lando Calrissian to go back to rescue him in the Millennium Falcon. In Return of the Jedi Han Solo is frozen and hanging on the wall as living art for Jabba the Hutt when Luke and Leia and the team come to rescue him.

In Harry Potter and the Sorcerer's Stone Firenze gives up the esteem of his fellow centaurs to rescue Harry from Voldemort/Quirrell in the Forbidden Forest. In Chamber of Secrets the Weasley boys rescue Harry in a flying car when he is locked in his bedroom by the Dursleys. In Goblet of Fire, Harry rescues underwater hostages during the Triwizard Tournament, putting their well-being above his goal of winning the tournament.

One of the most touching stories of rescue in the Harry Potter series is in The Order of the Phoenix, when Hagrid rescues his half-brother Grawp from the other giants, against Grawp's will and at risk of great personal injury. Hagrid endures severe physical injuries caused by Grawp, the wrath of forest creatures, questioning stares from colleagues and the skepticism of friends, but he was determined to free Grawp from a terrible life and bring him to live in the forbidden forest. Hagrid shows his brother great patience, believing the best in him and choosing to love him despite his dangerous and uncivilized behavior. It is not until the end of Harry's sixth year in *The Half-Blood Prince* that Hagrid's efforts appear to pay off; Grawp's social skills progress enough that he behaves himself at a funeral. His rescue is complete; his redemption still in process.

RESURRECTIONS

Han Solo is frozen alive in *Star Wars: The Empire Strikes Back*. We worried he might not survive, but he is resuscitated in *Return of the Jedi*. There are also more spiritual kinds of resurrections in *Star Wars*: Obi-Wan Kenobi dies in battle against Darth Vader but later reappears to Luke in spirit form. The finishing touch on the resurrection theme in *Star Wars* comes when Luke persuades his father, still Darth Vader, to turn from the dark side. Vader kills the Emperor and dies to save Luke. Like Obi-Wan and Yoda, he is not lost but lives on in the spirit realm, no longer as Darth Vader in his dark helmet and robes, but transformed into the restored Jedi Anakin Skywalker.

In Narnia, especially in *The Lion, the Witch and the Wardrobe* we see an actual resurrection from the dead. Aslan is killed by the White Witch, fulfilling the requirement of the Deep Magic and ransoming the life of the guilty Edmund. He then comes back to life in his physical body, although in a greater form. Susan and Lucy don't fully understand when they see Aslan resurrected; they aren't sure they can trust their eyes. But Aslan's resurrection is the first of many. He goes on to restore life to all the creatures that the witch had turned into stone. Aslan's resurrection power also infuses nature with new life: the spirits of the trees, the river god and others in the natural and spiritual realms are awakened.

There are also metaphorical resurrections in the Chronicles of Narnia. For example, in *The Silver Chair* we see Prince Rilian trapped in enchanted slavery to the Lady of the Green Kirtle. He is kept underground where he is as good as dead to his true self. When his enchantment is broken he rises up from the underworld to begin a new life in his rightful royal position.

At the end of *The Silver Chair* Eustace and Jill, children from our world, witness the resurrection of King Caspian, but only in Aslan's Country, not in ours or in Narnia. Caspian then asks to have a glimpse of Eustace and Jill's world but wonders if this is a wrong desire. Aslan reassures him: "You cannot want wrong things any more, now that you have died, my son." What a wonderful glimpse what life may be like after our resurrection when evil has been eliminated! Try to imagine a life where all our desires are right and good. That makes me look forward to resurrection!

The theme of resurrection comes up several times in *Harry Potter* as well. In *The Chamber of Secrets* while fighting the Basilisk to save Ginny, Harry is pierced by its poisonous fang. Anyone pierced with that fang should die. Tom Riddle even gloats, "You're dead Harry Potter," but Harry is resuscitated when Fawkes the Phoenix weeps on his wound. The restorative powers of the phoenix—a mythic symbol of resurrection—restored Harry to life. Meanwhile, having allowed Tom Riddle to pour himself into her through his enchanted diary, Ginny Weasley is as good as dead. However, Harry destroys Tom Riddle's diary, freeing Ginny from impending death and awakening her. So Ginny is raised up by Harry's intervention while she is, so to speak, "dead in her own trespasses and sins"—caught in a trap she willingly entered. Harry, Ginny, Ron and Professor Lockhart are then carried back to life above not by their own effort but by the Fawkes the phoenix—a classic symbol of resurrection.

RESURRECTION STORIES FROM THE BIBLE

There is a clear connection between the resurrection themes in mythic stories and resurrection in the Bible. Some think this is because the Bible is just myth and not true. But C. S. Lewis believed that resurrection themes hint at the "true myth" revealed in the resurrection of Jesus Christ. "He sent the human race what I call good dreams: I mean those queer stories scattered through the heathen religions about a god who dies and comes to life again and, by his death, has somehow given new life to men."[1]

There are several miraculous occurrences of resurrection in both Old and New Testaments. One I find very funny. The prophet Elisha—who had been very powerful and actually performed a resurrection—died and was buried in a cave.

> Moabite raiders used to enter the country every spring. Once while some Israelites were burying a man, suddenly they saw a band of raiders; so they threw the man's body into Elisha's tomb. When the body touched Elisha's bones, the man came to life and stood up on his feet. (2 Kings 13:20-21)

Imagine the scene from the corpse's point of view. Who knows what he was aware of while his dead body was tossed into the nearest tomb? However, a moment came when he was alive again and found himself in a cave with a skeleton touching him. The story leaves off with him coming to life and standing on his feet. I imagine he tore out of there as fast as he could. I wonder what kind of stories he was able to tell at the end of that day? Those of us who have experienced some sort of resurrection, especially if we have been raised from an old life of sin and death should run to tell others of the renewed life God has given us.

The most significant resurrection in the Bible is the resurrection of Jesus. This story can be read in differing versions toward the end of all four Gospels: Matthew, Mark, Luke and John. According to one account,

Jesus appeared alive after his resurrection to over five hundred witnesses. Another time he joined two followers for dinner. Before they realized who he was, he had spent the afternoon explaining to them how the Old Testament predicted that the Christ would have to die and rise from the dead. He gave a blessing for the food and then disappeared!

This belief in Jesus' resurrection was deemed worth dying for; the apostles and many of those who saw him after his resurrection went on to die for their testimony to that fact. The resurrection of Jesus stands at the center of the Christian faith, but what does this have to do with our ongoing personal journey and battles against evil?

There is another level to the resurrection life of Jesus; it is the new life Jesus gives to those he has raised up from the depths of their own sin and its deadly consequences. Consider the parallels between Ginny's resurrection, and the description of spiritual resurrection from the book of Ephesians: "As for you, you were dead in your transgressions and sin"—as Ginny was—"in which you used to live when you followed the ways of this world and of the ruler of the kingdom of the air, the spirit who is now at work in those who are disobedient."

> All of us also lived among them at one time, gratifying the cravings of our sinful nature and following its desires and thoughts. Like the rest, we were by nature objects of wrath. But because of his great love for us, God, who is rich in mercy, made us alive with Christ even when we were dead in transgressions—it is by grace you have been saved. And God raised us up with Christ and seated us with him in the heavenly realms in Christ Jesus, in order that in the coming ages he might show the incomparable riches of his grace, expressed in his kindness to us in Christ Jesus. (Ephesians 2:1-7)

REDEMPTION

Redemption is someone's freedom that has in some way been secured by another. The idea of redemption is often thought of in religious terms. However, even those unfamiliar with the sacrifice of Jesus Christ on the cross may be familiar with the concept of redemption from stories of fantastic fiction.

We see the beauty and power of redemption in *Harry Potter* when Lily Potter gave her life to save Harry. She chose to put herself in the way of the curse so Harry would have life. She didn't live to see it, but giving her life for his broke the power of the curse of death and gave Harry back his life. Such redemptive love was more powerful than Voldemort's most powerful weapon and utterly befuddled him. Harry lived on to love those who were held in bondage, like Dobby the house-elf. So the power of redemptive love carried on to bring life to Harry and freedom to Dobby.

In *The Lion, the Witch and the Wardrobe* Aslan has a conversation with the traitorous Edmund, frees him from the clutches of the witch and ultimately restores him as an heir to the throne of Narnia. In *Star Wars: Return of the Jedi,* Luke offers Darth Vader a second chance to save someone in his family, after his failed attempt to save Padmé left him abandoned to the dark side. Vader rescues his son, Luke, from the Emperor, knowing that it will probably cost him his life. But while his sacrifice saves Luke from death, Luke's invitation also saves Vader. Luke tries to get his father to safety but is stopped when his father asks him to remove his mask. Luke protests, "I have to save you," but his father replies, "You already have." Darth Vader, the former Anakin Skywalker, completes his journey out of the underworld of darkness and takes his place in the spirit realm with Yoda and Obi-Wan Kenobi, not resurrected physically but redeemed thoroughly.

LIFE AFTER LIFE

Encounters with those "resurrected" into the spirit realm, such as Yoda, Obi-Wan and Anakin but also the resurrected Prince Caspian and the released spirits of Harry Potter's parents in *The Goblet of Fire,* are reminiscent of something the Bible describes in the book of Hebrews. It refers to those who lived and died believing in God and his promises:

> Therefore, since we are surrounded by such a great cloud of witnesses, let us throw off everything that hinders and the sin that so easily entangles, and let us run with perseverance the race marked out for us. (Hebrews 12:1)

The implication is that those who have gone before are not really gone from us; they are watching us continue, and we have the recollection of their faith to motivate us to do our very best. Those who have experienced grand rescues, resurrection and redemption should likewise take our place among the great cloud of witnesses, telling our stories of deliverance that people need to hear and praying fervently and persistently for those who need to be rescued. Darth Vader's redemption stands as a symbol of hope that it is never too late. As long as there is life there is hope.

Sometimes in fantasy stories, there can be hope even when it looks like it's too late. That is because such stories have the ability to take us beyond the bounds of time. We will look at living beyond the bounds of time and the power of prophecy in our next chapter.

14

Beyond the Bounds of Time and Power of Prophecy

"When Adam's flesh and Adam's bone
Sits at Cair Paravel in throne,
The evil time will be over and done."

Narnian prophecy, The Lion, the Witch and the Wardrobe

Have you ever wondered why breaking beyond the bounds of time is a common theme in fantasy stories? Whether it's traveling with our heroes at light speed when escaping an enemy ship in *Star Wars*, wondering why Narnian time sometimes goes slowly in comparison to our world and on other occasions Narnia goes through hundreds of years in just one year between the children's visits, or seeing Hermione use a Time Turner to add more hours to her day, we see our fascination with overcoming the limitations of time.

Most fantasy stories also include prophecy, usually predicting the coming hero (or heroes) who will overcome evil and put the world right again. Such foretelling makes it seem as if a cosmic narrator, some Great Storyteller, knows the end from the beginning and reassures us that things will turn out for the good. It also invites the characters to help fulfill the prophecies by acting in keeping with them.

Perhaps our fascination with time can be explained by remembering the eternal nature of God and our creation in his image. King Solomon—called by the Bible the wisest man who ever lived—wrote that God "has made everything beautiful in its time. He has also set eternity in the hearts of men; yet they cannot fathom what God has done from beginning to end" (Ecclesiastes 3:11). Think back to the Bible's account of Adam and Eve in the Garden of Eden. They weren't created to die, but God warned them that disobedience would lead to death.

> And the LORD God commanded the man, "You are free to eat from any tree in the garden; but you must not eat from the tree of the knowledge of good and evil, for when you eat of it you will surely die." (Genesis 2:16-17)

We learn further on that God's original plan included living forever by eating from the tree of life. But Adam and Eve fell for the deception of the evil one and ate forbidden fruit from the tree of the knowledge of good and evil (and we have been reading stories about the battle between good and evil ever since). Their disobedience created quite a stir:

> The LORD God banished [Adam, with Eve] from the Garden of Eden to work the ground from which he had been taken. After he drove the man out, he placed on the east side of the Garden of Eden cherubim and a flaming sword flashing back and forth to guard the way to the tree of life. (Genesis 3:23-24)

They didn't drop dead the moment they ate the forbidden fruit, but that act started the clock ticking, counting down to death, life running out second by second. Ever wonder why God put the guard between them and the tree of life? I think it's because the curse of death required a remedy to corruption and decay. Otherwise forever living would mean forever dying, a curse of eternal proportions rather than the blessing God intended.

A quest began for eternal youth, for the power to turn back time, for immortality and the power to control the relentless march of time. Henry Wadsworth Longfellow put it this way in his poem *A Psalm of Life:*

Art is long, and Time is fleeting,
And our hearts, though stout and brave,
Still, like muffled drums, are beating
Funeral marches to the grave.

Human beings are not entirely comfortable within the constraints of linear time. While time marches on, people wish, *If only I could go back and do that over! If only I could take back what I said! If only I were young again!* So we make up stories to help us. In stories like *Star Wars* we see time mastered mechanically, flipping a switch that bends time to our heroes' will. In stories like *Harry Potter* we see time mastered magically, manipulating the elements of time to our heroes' advantage. In stories like Narnia we see time mastered mysteriously, observing the impact on our heroes' world of an existence lying outside the bounds of time.

We can't quite predict what time may do in the Chronicles of Narnia. When Jill and Eustace arrive in Narnia at the beginning of *The Silver Chair,* Aslan tells Jill that Eustace will see an old and dear friend. Eustace doesn't take into account that about seventy Narnian years have passed since he last saw his friend Prince Caspian. The young vibrant man he remembers has turned into a frail *old* man, King Caspian, who is facing death before he and his lost son have been properly reconciled.

The Narnian stories carry us further beyond the bounds of time, past King Caspian's death into Aslan's country, where Jill and Eustace can still hear the funeral dirge. The children are then transported to the mountains of Aslan's country, above and beyond the end of the world in which Narnia lies. They still hear funeral music for the dead king while in Aslan's presence. In a crystal-clear, beautiful stream with golden gravel they see water flowing over Caspian's dead body. "All three stood and wept. Even the Lion wept: great Lion-tears, each tear more precious than the Earth would be if it were a solid diamond." Aslan sends Eustace to pluck a sharp thorn and drive it into his paw. Although reluctant, Eustace obeys. A great drop of blood from the Lion's paw splashes into the stream over the king's dead body, the funeral music stops, and the dead King immediately begins to change. His beard, white with age, retreats and becomes yellow. His face loses its pallor and flushes full of life. His body regains its full health. Caspian opens his eyes, springs from the water and stands before them, fully alive beyond the bounds of time.

How does our seeing the limitations of time overcome in fantasy stories help us in our own daily lives, and more broadly in our own hero's journey? There are several things we can learn.

PRACTICE SEEING WITH EYES OF FAITH

At the end of *Harry Potter and the Prisoner of Azkaban*, Dumbledore suggests Hermione and Harry use the Time Turner to go back in time three hours in order to save Buckbeak from execution and Sirius Black from losing his soul to the Dementors. Harry and Hermione experience the terrifying hours of Buckbeak's execution twice: two times they are taken into the Shrieking Shack with Ron, Sirius Black, Professor Lupin, Peter Pettigrew and Professor Snape; they see the moon come out and Lupin transform into a werewolf; they watch Pettigrew escape and the Dementors swoop down on Harry and Sirius. The reader is frightened at the prospect that they may both lose their souls. The first time through, they don't know what will happen or who will survive, but Harry looks across the lake and sees someone who looks like his father conjure the Patronus spell to rescue them. The second time, Harry realizes that *he* had conjured the Patronus. Having already seen himself do it, this time around he knows he can and therefore finds the necessary confidence.

This story raises interesting thoughts for me about faith. The Bible says faith is powerful; with faith we can move mountains! "Faith is the substance of things hoped for, the evidence of things not seen" (Hebrews 11:1 KJV). Faith is, in a way, seeing something internally as if what we hope for has already happened—playing fast and loose with linear time. Confidently acting in faith, then, is a way of breaking beyond the bounds of time. Faith is like fast-forwarding hope, or rewinding fact. As the Bible puts it, "We live by faith, not by sight" (2 Corinthians 5:7). We need to learn to see with "eyes of faith."

The Patronus spell is conjured when wizards think of their happiest thought and say, "Expecto Patronum." The word *Patronum* or Patronus is reminiscent of its Latin root word *Pater,* which means father, and Harry's Patronus looks like a stag—the form his father took as his animagus. Harry, we understand, is calling on his father for help and protection.

Jesus taught that we have the privilege of calling on God as "Abba" Father and asking him to help us when we face troubles. We are told to pray to our Father in heaven; he is always ready to come to our aid and protect us when our souls are in danger. So through prayer, we are able to alter the course of the future in keeping with God's will for our lives. We can have a firm expectation of an answer in the physical realm that will remedy the danger of the present situation and change the future so good will triumph over evil. This too is a way of breaking beyond the bounds of time to get help in our times of need.

C. S. Lewis shows "Father Time" to be Aslan's servant; it is at Aslan's command that Narnian time winds down and the friends of Aslan move beyond the bounds of time. At the end of *The Last Battle* Aslan awakens the great giant Father Time by his roar, who then blows a horn that causes the stars to fall from the sky, and Narnia comes to an end. There is a certain comfort in reading and rereading the Chronicles of Narnia; you can think back to when Aslan gave his life as a sacrifice to save Edmund from the hand of the White Witch. You can recall that the Stone Table upon which the Deep Magic was written broke in two, and death itself started working backward. You can look forward to *The Last Battle* when Narnia is wrapped up and put away, making way for all the friends of Aslan to enter happily into Aslan's country, and note that despite his treachery, Edmund is no less a king of Narnia than any other. Navigating back and forth through the timeline of the stories, you can know that in the end all the sins and mistakes of the past are forgiven and left behind, remedied by Aslan's sacrifice, and that moving forward in the stories, good repeatedly and finally triumphs over evil.

This idea of navigating back and forth in time, from past history we believe, to the present and into the future that has been predicted, is what life should be like for people who believe the Bible. We can trust the One who (like Aslan) lives beyond the bounds of time and ultimately controls time. Through the Bible God tells us the important things that happened in the past, how to deal with life today, and important things that will certainly happen in the future with regard to the overall battle between good and evil. Consider the time frames and tenses used in the following passage penned by the apostle Paul to his protégé Timothy. Paul breaks beyond the bounds of time by faith to gain assurance he needs to deal with present suffering:

> This grace was given us in Christ Jesus *before the beginning of time* [past], but it has *now been revealed* [present] through the appearing of our Savior, Christ Jesus, who *has destroyed* death and *has brought* life and immortality [past] to light through the gospel. And of this gospel I *was appointed* [past] a herald and an apostle and a teacher. That is why I *am suffering* [present] as I am. Yet I am not ashamed, because I *know* [present] whom I *have believed* [past], and *am convinced* [present] that he is able to guard what I have entrusted to him *for that day* [future]. (2 Timothy 1:9-12)

As with Aslan in Narnia, God in our world has complete rule over past, present and future time. He is eternal and even knows the end from the beginning. Indeed the Bible declares that Jesus Christ is the same yesterday, today and forever.

THE POWER OF PROPHECY IN FANTASY STORIES

Fantastic stories usually include an element of prophecy, predicting the coming one or ones who will overthrow evil and put their world to rights. In *Harry Potter* we learn of a prophecy of one who will have the power to destroy Voldemort, a prophecy Voldemort takes to refer to Harry. *Star Wars* features a prophecy that a Jedi (Anakin Skywalker) will defeat the Sith and bring balance back to the force. In *The Lion, the Witch and the Wardrobe* a prophecy predicts that two sons of Adam and two daughters of Eve will take the four thrones at Cair Paravel and end the reign of the White Witch, along with her cursed winter. Another prophecy predicts:

> Wrong will be right, when Aslan comes in sight,
> At the sound of his roar, sorrows will be no more,
> When he bears his teeth, winter meets its death
> And when he shakes his mane, we shall have spring again.

It's not just these three fantasy stories; almost all fantasy stories include a prophecy of a coming one who will overthrow evil, break the curse, free those in bondage and bring jubilation. In short, most fantasy stories provide readers with a promised savior or messiah figure. Again, why? I believe God created us with a longing for a Savior, one who can undo the damage of sin that goes back to Adam and Eve. We long for one who will remedy the evil in our world and in ourselves. We long for this because God designed it into the story of our lives.

From beginning to end, the Bible is full of prophecies of a coming one who would overthrow evil with good, free us from the tyranny of sin and death, and give us eternal life. The Old Testament or Hebrew Scriptures could be condensed into a summary: He is coming! The New Testament could be summed up as: He has come! And he will come again to finish the story!

Starting in the Garden of Eden, shortly after Adam and Eve fall into sin, God predicted the destruction of the evil one by the offspring of a woman:

> And I will put enmity
>> between you and the woman,
>> and between your offspring and hers;
> he will crush your head,
>> and you will strike his heel. (Genesis 3:15)

God gave Moses, the great lawgiver and deliverer of the Hebrews, a prophecy:

> I will raise up for them a prophet like you from among their brothers; I will put my words in his mouth, and he will tell them everything I command him. If anyone does not listen to my words that the prophet speaks in my name, I myself will call him to account. (Deuteronomy 18:18-19)

King David also recorded prophecies about the savior who would come through his descendants. We read a graphic description of the crucifixion in his Psalm 22, even down to the details of the soldiers casting lots for his clothing.

The prophet Isaiah predicted:

> For to us a child is born,
>> to us a son is given,
>> and the government will be on his shoulders.
> And he will be called
>> Wonderful Counselor, Mighty God,
>> Everlasting Father, Prince of Peace.
> Of the increase of his government and peace

there will be no end.
He will reign on David's throne
    and over his kingdom,
establishing and upholding it
    with justice and righteousness
    from that time on and forever.
The zeal of the LORD Almighty
    will accomplish this. (Isaiah 9:6-7)

Isaiah also predicted that the coming one would take a surprising form and be misunderstood. Isaiah 53 reads like a riddle, predicting before the time of Christ a coming one who would suffer to pay for our sins even while we considered him stricken by God.

Yet it was the LORD's will to crush him and cause him to suffer,
    and though the LORD makes his life a guilt offering,
he will see his offspring and prolong his days,
    and the will of the LORD will prosper in his hand.
After the suffering of his soul,
    he will see the light of life and be satisfied;
by his knowledge my righteous servant will justify many,
    and he will bear their iniquities.
Therefore I will give him a portion among the great,
    and he will divide the spoils with the strong,
because he poured out his life unto death,
    and was numbered with the transgressors.
For he bore the sin of many,
    and made intercession for the transgressors. (Isaiah 53:10-12)

Early believers in Jesus used the Old Testament prophecies to argue that Jesus was the promised and anticipated "coming one." The New Testament (especially the Gospel of Matthew) explains how Jesus Christ fulfilled those prophecies and offers more prophecies about how he will come again to finish the job of overthrowing evil and establishing his good, just and righteous kingdom. Peter's first stirring sermon explains this:

> Jesus of Nazareth was a man accredited by God to you by miracles, wonders and signs, which God did among you through him, as you yourselves know. This man was handed over to you by God's set purpose and foreknowledge; and you, with the help of wicked men, put him to death by nailing him to the cross. But God raised him from the dead, freeing him from the agony of death, because it was impossible for death to keep its hold on him. David said about him:
>
> "I saw the Lord always before me.
>> Because he is at my right hand,
>> I will not be shaken.
> Therefore my heart is glad and my tongue rejoices;
>> my body also will live in hope,
> because you will not abandon me to the grave,
>> nor will you let your Holy One see decay.
> You have made known to me the paths of life;
>> you will fill me with joy in your presence."
>
> Brothers, I can tell you confidently that the patriarch David died and was buried, and his tomb is here to this day. But he was a prophet and knew that God had promised him on oath that he would place one of his descendants on his throne. Seeing what was ahead, he spoke of the resurrection of the Christ, that he was not abandoned to the grave, nor did his body see decay. God has raised this Jesus to life, and we are all witnesses of the fact. Exalted to the right hand of God, he has received from the Father the promised

Holy Spirit and has poured out what you now see and hear. For David did not ascend to heaven, and yet he said,

"The Lord said to my Lord:
    'Sit at my right hand
until I make your enemies
    a footstool for your feet.'"

Therefore let all Israel be assured of this: God has made this Jesus, whom you crucified, both Lord and Christ. (Acts 2:22-36)

THE GREAT STORYTELLER WHO KNOWS ALL THE DETAILS IN ADVANCE

There is one more reason we respond to prophecy. The fulfillment of prophecies validates God's omniscience. Very specific prophecies—even down to naming names—are woven throughout Scripture and have blown away astounding odds by coming true. God himself points to fulfilled prophecy as proof he alone is God. Isaiah 44:6-7 declares,

This is what the LORD says—Israel's King and Redeemer, the LORD of Heaven's armies:

"I am the First and the Last;
    there is no other God.
Who else is like me?
    Let him step forward and prove to you his power.
Let him do as I have done since ancient times
    when I established a people and explained its future." (NLT)

The Bible tells us that we are to always be ready to given an answer for the hope that is within us. Fulfilled prophecy is one of my favorite reasons for hope not only that God's word is true, but also that God the Great Storyteller knows our stories generations before we are born.

More than seven hundred years before Christ, the prophet Isaiah predicted that the Jews living in Israel would be taken into captivity and that Jerusalem, along with the temple, would be destroyed. However, the prophecy of Isaiah also predicted a time of restoration and even gave the name of the unbelieving king who would authorize rebuilding the Temple and Jerusalem. God

> says of Cyrus, "He is my shepherd and will accomplish all that I please; he will say of Jerusalem, 'Let it be rebuilt,' and of the temple, 'Let its foundations be laid.'" (Isaiah 44:28)

Remember, when Isaiah recorded this Jerusalem was a thriving city and the temple the bustling center of Jewish society. The prophecy continues:

> This is what the LORD says to his anointed,
>   to Cyrus, whose right hand I take hold of
> to subdue nations before him
>   and to strip kings of their armor,
> to open doors before him
>   so that gates will not be shut:
> I will go before you
>   and will level the mountains;
> I will break down gates of bronze
>   and cut through bars of iron.
> I will give you the treasures of darkness,
>   riches stored in secret places,
> so that you may know that I am the LORD,
>   the God of Israel, *who summons you by name.*
> For the sake of Jacob my servant,
>   of Israel my chosen,
> *I summon you by name*
>   and bestow on you a title of honor,
>   *though you do not acknowledge me.* (Isaiah 45:1-4)

Why would God use Cyrus and predict his name generations in advance? So people could know the God of the Bible is Lord:

> Apart from me there is no God.
> I will strengthen you,
>> *though you have not acknowledged me,*
> so that from the rising of the sun
>> to the place of its setting
> men may know there is none besides me.
> I am the LORD, and there is no other. (Isaiah 45:5-6)

On January 15, 588 B.C., Babylon overthrew the nation of Judah and its capital Jerusalem, deporting many. On July 28, 586 B.C., Jerusalem and the temple were destroyed by Babylon and the treasures taken to Babylon. History records that the last native rulers of Babylon were Nabonidus and his son Belshazzar. They were overthrown by *Cyrus,* king of Persia, who crossed the Tigris *from the east* (also predicted) to enter Babylon in October 539 B.C. Cyrus had a policy of cooperating with local religions and allowing the return of exiles. He found the hidden treasures of Israel that had been taken by Babylon and declared the rebuilding of Jerusalem and the temple. This is all confirmed by archaeology and inscriptions of King Cyrus. More important, this was all precisely as God predicted over 162 years before Cyrus of Persia was born!

The Bible records this fulfillment of Isaiah's and Jeremiah's prophecies:

> In the first year of Cyrus king of Persia, in order to fulfill the word of the LORD spoken by Jeremiah, the LORD moved the heart of Cyrus king of Persia to make a proclamation throughout his realm and to put it in writing:
>
>> "This is what Cyrus king of Persia says: 'The LORD, the God of heaven, has given me all the kingdoms of the earth and he has appointed me to build a temple for him at Jerusalem in Judah.

Anyone of his people among you—may the LORD his God be
with him, and let him go up.'" (2 Chronicles 36:22-23)

So we see God's use of predictive prophecy to provide evidence that he
alone is God, dwelling beyond the bounds of time.

PROPHECY AND FREE WILL

In many fantastic stories, prophecies drive the story forward. However,
it is interesting to consider the role predictive prophecies played in motivating characters on the side of good and evil. In *Star Wars: The Empire
Strikes Back* Luke is face down in the snow, in danger of death, having
just escaped from the snow monster's cave. Obi-Wan Kenobi appears to
him and utters: "You will go to the Dagoba system. There you will learn
from Yoda, the Jedi Master who instructed me." What might be taken as
a command has a prophetic tone in that Obi Wan says "you will." This
gives Luke hope that his life won't end there. It was still up to Luke to
actually go to the Dagoba system and seek Yoda, which he did. This in
turn helped fulfill the prophecy.

C. S. Lewis used prophecies to show how free will and destiny work
together. The prophecy of the sons of Adam and daughters of Eve bringing the White Witch's downfall ended up being fulfilled, but it also gen-
erated the White Witch's plan to kill Edmund. Aslan, who knew the
prophecies, was confident all would work out for the good.

In *The Voyage of the "Dawn Treader"* a dryad's prophecy—given over
Reepicheep as a baby mouse—predicted his destiny but also encouraged
him to fulfill it. Knowing the prophecy, and sensing he was destined for
this great end, gave him the courage to continue sailing to the utter East.

In *Harry Potter and the Half-Blood Prince* J. K. Rowling explores interesting questions about the power of acting on one's belief in a prophecy.
We see that a prophecy given by Sybil Trelawney prompted Voldemort
to go to Godric's Hollow on Halloween night to kill Harry's father and

Harry using the Avada Kedavra spell. This turned out to validate the prophecy by marking Harry as his equal. Voldemort's *belief* in the prophecy set in motion the events that caused Harry to resolve to kill Voldemort or die trying.

Even though God *knows* and can predict what will happen, the Bible still leaves room for each person's free will in responding to God's word and the Savior he sent. The prophecies are written in the Bible; we are to believe them and act on them. Even though God's stories are full of prophecies, we are expected to use our intelligence to evaluate any prophecy claiming to be from God. There are people who say they speak prophecies from God today; we are to judge their words by the Bible and by whether their predictions come true. We are to reject fortune telling of any kind that is not from the Holy Spirit, and respond freely to prophecy to move forward in our journey.

Time and Eternity

Most Bible stories are laboriously set in their historical context, carefully recording genealogies, locations and political leaders. However, other Bible comments made within linear time give us glimpses into eternity past and eternity future. One account even says that time stood still (Joshua 10:12-13). Some things Jesus said show he lived beyond the bounds of time. At the Last Supper, Jesus prayed for his followers. "Father, the time has come." Jesus was firmly grounded in time, but the gift he then prays for is definitely beyond the bounds of time: "Glorify your Son, that your Son may glorify you. For you granted him authority over all people that he might give eternal life to all those you have given him. . . . I have brought you glory on earth by completing the work you gave me to do. And now, Father, glorify me in your presence with the glory I had with you *before the world began*" (John 17:1-5). Jesus' claim to have lived with God the Father before the world began is definitely beyond the bounds of time.

John's Gospel opens with this declaration of Christ's preexistence: "In the beginning was the Word, and the Word was with God, and the Word was God. He was with God in the beginning" (John 1:1-2). Here we see Christ existing before time began; yet the writer to the Hebrews asserts that "Jesus Christ is the same yesterday and today and forever" (Hebrews 13:8).

Perhaps we love stories that take us beyond the bounds of time because they take us where God created us to live, with an awareness of eternity. This helps us bear our sufferings now, forgive the sins of the past, and look forward with confident hope to the future when God, who is eternal, will take us literally beyond the bounds of time. We take up the final judgment and eternity in the next chapter.

15

Rewards and Just Desserts

"'Dear me,' . . . 'Impaled upon your own sword, Gilderoy!'
'Sword?' said Lockhart dimly. 'Haven't got a sword.'
'That boy has though.' He pointed at Harry. 'He'll lend
you one.'"

Dumbledore and Professor Lockhart,
Harry Potter and the Chamber of Secrets

One of the things we love about fantastic fiction is that the stories end in a very satisfying way. Once the hero team has conquered in the ultimate battle or finished their quest, the time comes for justice to be served, wrongs to be righted and punishment meted out to the unrepentant devotees of evil. Glory goes to the victors and disgrace or destruction to those who hold tightly to evil. Good triumphs and characters generally get what's coming to them.

This kind of wrap-up satisfies our innate sense of justice and—I think—also makes up for the times in real life when things don't seem to turn out the way we think is fair. Stories help bridge the gap until such a time when our own world will be set right, evil defeated, wrongdoers punished and rewards given.

PUNISHMENT FOR UNREPENTANT EVIL

The nice thing about a story is that we have a chance to see characters progress over the course of time. Often we see them go to the end of their lives so that we can consider the course of their lives as a whole and the ultimate consequences of their choices. Readers of fantastic fiction don't mind seeing a repentant evil-doer freed from punishment, as in the case of Ginny Weasley in *Harry Potter and the Chamber of Secrets,* Darth Vader in *Star Wars: Return of the Jedi* or Puzzle the Narnian donkey in *The Last Battle.* However, most readers or viewers would be disappointed if the story ended without the unrepentant getting their just deserts.

Many times we will be able to see that the bad that happens to a character receiving punishment grows directly out of their wrongdoing. This serves as a lesson for the hero team and illustrates a truth the Bible teaches in Galatians 6:7-9:

> Do not be deceived: God cannot be mocked. A man reaps what he sows. The one who sows to please his sinful nature, from that nature will reap destruction; the one who sows to please the Spirit, from the Spirit will reap eternal life. Let us not become weary in doing good, for at the proper time we will reap a harvest if we do not give up.

Some sins bring their own punishment or call for a reaction that should have been predictable were it not for the villain's blind spot: lust for power, prejudice, selfish ambition, vanity, and so on. The lesson for those seeking to do good is that *if we persist* in doing good we will *eventually* reap a rewarding harvest. In the meantime, we can enjoy a good story where we get to see characters like Jabba the Hutt in *Star Wars,* Uncle Andrew in *The Magician's Nephew* and Professor Umbrage in *Harry Potter and the Order of the Phoenix* reap the dark harvest of their dark ways.

In *Star Wars: Return of the Jedi* Jabba the Hutt forces Princess Leia into a skimpy outfit and chains her to him. She turns around and strangles him when the battle breaks out. He put her there, he gave her the chain, and he got what he deserved.

In *The Magician's Nephew* Uncle Andrew is selfish, greedy for power, self-aggrandizing and enamored with evil. He goes through a series of dark magical experiments to turn the dust from Atlantis into magical rings that would carry someone into an unknown land. He forces Digory and Polly out of this world, but he faces all kinds of trouble when they return to London with Jadis. "At the first sign of disobedience," she threatens him, "I will lay such spells on you that anything you sit down on will feel like red hot iron and whenever you lie in a bed there will be invisible blocks of ice at your feet." He brought this hardship on himself.

Even people on the good side have to bear the consequences for wrongdoing. One of the best examples of this is found in *The Horse and His Boy*. Aravis manages to give her servant girl something to knock her out so that Aravis can escape. She doesn't think of the whipping the girl receives for allowing her to escape. Later in the story, a lion swipes at Aravis with its claws and lacerates her back. Aslan eventually reveals to Shasta and Aravis that he is the only lion they ever encountered; we realize that the lacerations Aravis received are equal to the lacerations borne by her servant girl because Aravis drugged her and escaped.

In *Harry Potter and the Order of the Phoenix,* Delores Jane Umbrage, professor of Defense Against the Dark Arts during Harry's fifth year at Hogwarts, is a bastion of bigotry, despising and demeaning anyone considered half-blood or half-breed. She treats Hagrid like a dunce because he is part-giant. Hermione—knowing Umbrage's bigotry—anticipates how she will treat centaurs and lures her into a situation where she would reap the consequences of her own dark nature. Umbrage is surrounded by about fifty centaurs in the forbidden forest and tells them, "By the laws laid down by the Department for the Regulation and Control of Magical Creatures, any attack by half-breeds such as yourselves on a human . . ." She proceeds to say they have "near-human intelligence" and offers other insults, screaming "Filthy half-breeds!" as they threaten violence. With that, she is carried off by a mob of angry centaurs.

PUNISHMENT MITIGATED BY MERCY

I must admit I was a bit disappointed Umbrage wasn't punished more thoroughly. I didn't want to see her come out of that forest alive, but that leads to an auxiliary point we often see in such stories: even with punishment there is still room for mercy. Professor Umbrage is not left to the centaurs; Dumbledore enters the forest alone to rescue her. He brings her back to the hospital wing and provides for her care, along with the others who have been hurt.

We see something similar with Gilderoy Lockhart, professor of Defense Against the Dark Arts teacher in *Harry Potter and the Chamber of Secrets*. Lockhart's dark streak took the form of vanity and selfish ambition. He went around the world collecting the experiences and knowledge of people who had really fought evil, using his wand and a memory charm to make them forget he had stolen their expertise. He attempts to use Ron's wand to erase Ron and Harry's memories and leave them in the Chamber of Secrets to die. But Ron's wand is broken, so the curse backfires against Lockhart. He deserved to have his memory obliviated, and we might have left it at that, but that's not where the author leaves it. In *Order of the Phoenix* Harry, Hermione and Ron discover Lockhart at St. Mungo's Hospital, on the ward for spell damage. Even though he hasn't changed much in character—he assumes they've come to get his autograph—nevertheless he is being cared for with compassion and mercy.

In the end, the author of a story decides who is forgiven and who is punished to varying degrees of severity. The author determines who will be shown mercy and who will be utterly destroyed. God, the author and finisher of our world's story, is the one who should and will mete out vengeance, mercy, punishments and rewards in our world. We are told this clearly in both Old and New Testaments. In Deuteronomy, God says,

> It is mine to avenge; I will repay. In due time their foot will slip;
> their day of disaster is near and their doom rushes upon them.
> The LORD will judge his people and have compassion on his servants. (Deuteronomy 32:35-36)

And in the apostle Paul's letter to the Romans, we're told:

> Do not take revenge, my friends, but leave room for God's wrath, for it is written: "It is mine to avenge; I will repay," says the Lord. On the contrary:
> > "If your enemy is hungry, feed him;
> > > if he is thirsty, give him something to drink.
> > In doing this, you will heap burning coals on his head."
> Do not be overcome by evil, but overcome evil with good.
> (Romans 12:19-21)

God is in charge of repaying evil and bringing doom to those who deserve it. We can trust that God will bring about the requisite vengeance. He reminds us that we too are to be judged so that we appreciate God's compassion when it applies to us. Therefore, we are free to choose to do good to those who have done us wrong. This is a powerful way to overcoming evil.

Two principles can bolster us in our journey and help us perform rightly in our battles:

1. In the end, those who deserve vengeance will get it. In our stories a good author will make sure of it. In our lives, God will make sure of it, although we may not see it for ourselves. We don't have to worry.
2. There is always a place for vengeance to be mitigated with mercy, especially when the person or character is repentant, even if that comes at the last moment of their story. We don't know what will happen at the final moment, so we need to leave that to the author.

In the end, although earlier in the story we might have been just as happy if he had died a terrible death, we are happy to see Darth Vader turn away from the dark side and be redeemed. I'm reminded of the repentant criminal beside Jesus on the cross. He recognized his guilt, saying to the other criminal being crucified with them, "We are punished justly, for we are getting what our deeds deserve." He also acknowledged Jesus' innocence: "This man has done nothing wrong." Then he asked Jesus for mercy: "Jesus, remember me when you come into your kingdom." Jesus answered him, "I tell you the truth, today you will be with me in paradise."

We can trust that there will be punishment for the guilty, but we can also be encouraged that vengeance can be mitigated by mercy even at the last moment.

FINAL JUDGMENT

Fantastic stories allow the author to deal finally with individual characters and entire worlds. In *Star Wars: Return of the Jedi* we see the evil Emperor, Darth Sidius, thrown into a pit flashing with ominous explosions that surely depict the end of him. In *The Last Battle* of Narnia we see a form of judgment after death. King Tirian is forced into the stable and sees the manifestation of the god Tash, whom his enemies called on but did not believe in. When those same enemies are forced into the stable, Tash—with his vulture-head and numerous arms—carries them off as his rightful prey. We also see a detailed picture of the separation of all Narnia's inhabitants at the end of that world in *The Last Battle*. "On the grass before them lay their own shadows. But the great thing was Aslan's shadow. It streamed away to their left, enormous and very terrible."

> By thousands and by millions, came all kinds of creatures. . . . But as they came right up to Aslan one or other of two things happened to each of them. They all looked straight in his face. I don't think they had any choice about that. And when some looked the ex-

pression on their faces changed terribly—it was fear and hatred.
. . . All the creatures who looked at Aslan in that way swerved to
their right, his left, and disappeared into his huge black shadow,
which streamed away to the left of the doorway. The children never
saw them again. I don't know what became of them.

The Bible provides us a scene of final judgment, depicting what God
knows will happen at the conclusion of our world's story. Here in the
closing chapters of the book of Revelation we see spiritual and material,
natural and supernatural realms converge. People debate how much of
this is figurative or symbolic language, but either way it is a stark scene
of a final judgment against God's enemies:

I saw heaven standing open and there before me was a white horse,
whose rider is called Faithful and True. With justice he judges and
makes war. His eyes are like blazing fire, and on his head are many
crowns. He has a name written on him that no one knows but he
himself. He is dressed in a robe dipped in blood, and his name is
the Word of God.

The armies of heaven were following him, riding on white
horses and dressed in fine linen, white and clean. Out of his mouth
comes a sharp sword with which to strike down the nations. "He
will rule them with an iron scepter." He treads the winepress of the
fury of the wrath of God Almighty. On his robe and on his thigh he
has this name written:

KING OF KINGS AND LORD OF LORDS.

And I saw an angel standing in the sun, who cried in a loud voice
to all the birds flying in midair, "Come, gather together for the
great supper of God, so that you may eat the flesh of kings, generals, and mighty men, of horses and their riders, and the flesh of all
people, free and slave, small and great."

Then I saw the beast and the kings of the earth and their armies gathered together to make war against the rider on the horse and his army. But the beast was captured, and with him the false prophet who had performed the miraculous signs on his behalf. With these signs he had deluded those who had received the mark of the beast and worshiped his image. The two of them were thrown alive into the fiery lake of burning sulfur. The rest of them were killed with the sword that came out of the mouth of the rider on the horse, and all the birds gorged themselves on their flesh. (Revelation 19:11-21)

There is still the devil to deal with, the one who started all the evildoing on the earth, and who lured all those who ended up in rebellion against God to their destruction. John, the apostle who saw the vision, writes about what he saw after that:

And I saw an angel coming down out of heaven, having the key to the Abyss and holding in his hand a great chain. He seized the dragon, that ancient serpent, who is the devil, or Satan, and bound him for a thousand years. He threw him into the Abyss, and locked and sealed it over him, to keep him from deceiving the nations anymore until the thousand years were ended. After that, he must be set free for a short time. . . .

And [afterward] the devil, who deceived them, was thrown into the lake of burning sulfur, where the beast and the false prophet had been thrown. They will be tormented day and night for ever and ever. (Revelation 20:1-4, 10)

This final destruction of the evil one gives me great satisfaction, but it is mingled with sadness: the story shows that people who God did not want to perish will be destroyed along with the evil one.

Jesus tells a story about judgment in which sheep and goats are sorted. "He will say to those on his left, 'Depart from me, you who are cursed, into the eternal fire prepared for the devil and his angels'" (Matthew 25:41). God never wanted *people* to suffer such final judgment; that ultimate punishment was prepared for the devil and his fallen angels. At the beginning of our story, God didn't want us to even taste evil, or its deadly consequences. But, as our stories play out, those who cling to evil end up going to the place prepared for the evil one, even though God has done all to freely offer a way to heaven.

Yes, the Bible says there is a horrible place prepared for the devil and his angels, but Jesus has prepared a good place for us. It is a place where we are totally forgiven, blessed with only goodness and righteousness, a place where no evil will remain, a place where we will receive rewards.

REWARDS FOR THE FAITHFUL

Fans of fantastic fiction expect a happy ending. We want to see good rewarded. Think of the scenes at the end of your favorite stories. At the end of *The Lion, the Witch and the Wardrobe* Peter, Susan, Edmund and Lucy are honored by Aslan, fulfilling their destiny and becoming kings and queens in Narnia. In *The Voyage of the "Dawn Treader,"* Reepicheep is rewarded with the fulfillment of his prophecy. In *The Silver Chair* Prince Rilian makes it back to the overworld and is restored to his rightful position as king. In *The Horse and His Boy* Shasta discovers he is really the lost Prince Cor and is rewarded with wealth, power and his true destiny. As part of his reward, he marries Aravis.

I love the way George Lucas writes ending scenes in *Star Wars*. At the end of *A New Hope,* after helping bring about the destruction of the Death Star, Princess Leia is lauded and celebrated by her people as she is restored to her throne. Luke Skywalker, Han Solo and Chewbacca are honored, and everyone is happy. Then in *Return of the Jedi,* Han Solo and Lando Calrissian destroy the second Death Star and restore freedom to the galaxy. They are made generals, and everyone on the good side lines up with their arms around each other as if appearing for a curtain call. Even those in the spirit realm are included. Everyone is happy; that's how it's supposed to end.

I love the ending to *Harry Potter and the Sorcerer's Stone*. In the intense rivalry between Gryffindor and Slytherin, it appears that Slytherin has won the house cup while everyone on the hero team was risking their lives to protect the school from evil. The great hall is decorated in Slytherin's colors, with their banners bearing the snake hanging proudly and Harry's nemesis Draco Malfoy gloating with his crew. But at the final moment, Dumbledore awards Harry, Ron, Hermione and Neville points for their heroism in the quest to save the Sorcerer's Stone. In an instant the banners change from the green and silver of Slytherin to the red and gold of Gryffindor. Cheers break out at the Gryffindor table, and the reader rejoices that good has triumphed over evil once more.

The end of *Harry Potter and the Chamber of Secrets* is doubly satisfying: Dobby, Malfoy's ill-used house-elf who warns Harry of danger, is rewarded with his freedom when Harry tricks Lucius Malfoy into giving Dobby a sock—an article of clothing, the means of liberation for house-elfs. Meanwhile, Dumbledore is restored to his position as headmaster, and Hagrid is freed from wrongful imprisonment in Azkaban and returns happily to Hogwarts. All's well that ends well.

It's not only in fantasy stories where I expect to see rewards. The Bible shows us that God will give rewards. "I the LORD search the heart / and examine the mind, / to reward a man according to his conduct, / according to what his deeds deserve" (Jeremiah 17:10). Indeed, our faith is tied up with the expectation that following the Lord and seeking to please God will bring rewards. The book of Hebrews says, "Without faith it is impossible to please God, because anyone who comes to him must believe that he exists and that he rewards those who earnestly seek him" (Hebrews 11:6).

Scripture promises that people will reap what they sow. Proceeding diligently in the right direction will bring rewards in this life and in the one to come. Although there are times in the midst of life when bad things happen to good people, we have to trust that God will work that out in the end. We who trust the God of the Bible can rest assured that good hearts and deeds will eventually be rewarded. Similarly, even when we suffer the consequences of bad choices, we can still look forward: in the future the remnants of bad consequences will be gone, replaced by the fruits of obedience to God. According to the Bible, those who persistently follow the good path will receive future rewards that far outweigh the punishments of the past.

FINAL REWARDS

The final chapters of Revelation give astounding glimpses into God's eternal kingdom. It describes a city paved with gold, adorned with every imaginable precious stone. John relates the vision he saw:

> I did not see a temple in the city, because the Lord God Almighty and the Lamb are its temple. The city does not need the sun or the moon to shine on it, for the glory of God gives it light, and the Lamb is its lamp. The nations will walk by its light, and the kings of the earth will bring their splendor into it. On no day will its gates ever be shut, for there will be no night there. The glory and honor of the nations will be brought into it. Nothing impure will ever enter it, nor will anyone who does what is shameful or deceitful, but only those whose names are written in the Lamb's book of life. (Revelation 21:22-27)

This imagery of the Lamb is symbolic of Christ's role as the Passover lamb, dying to take away the sins of the world. But it also reminds fans of Narnia of the ending of *The Voyage of the "Dawn Treader."* Eustace, Edmund and Lucy reach the meadows on the shore of the seas at the world's end. There they meet a lamb who fixes them a meal at the seashore. The

Lamb turns into Aslan, who tells them that Edmund and Lucy will not be coming back to Narnia. They are saddened by the thought of no longer seeing Aslan, but he comforts them, saying that they must learn to know him by another name in their own world. Thus the Lamb in Narnia reminds us of the Lamb of God we see in the final pages of the Bible.

The passage in Revelation goes on to describe a place where nothing impure, nothing evil or deceitful will ever enter in.

> Then the angel showed me the river of the water of life, as clear as crystal, flowing from the throne of God and of the Lamb down the middle of the great street of the city. On each side of the river stood the tree of life, bearing twelve crops of fruit, yielding its fruit every month. And the leaves of the tree are for the healing of the nations. No longer will there be any curse. The throne of God and of the Lamb will be in the city, and his servants will serve him. They will see his face, and his name will be on their foreheads. There will be no more night. They will not need the light of a lamp or the light of the sun, for the Lord God will give them light. And they will reign for ever and ever. (Revelation 22:1-5)

This scene is full of promise for the final rewards of those on God's side. The tree of life in this scene had been in the Garden of Eden, guarded by an angel with a flaming sword after Adam and Eve ate forbidden fruit from the tree of the knowledge of good and evil. In the final scene of God's true and fantastic story, God's people are once again given the fruit of eternal life. Evil is taken away, only good will go on, and God will wipe away every tear. No more sickness, nor pain, nor death. The curse is no more. The light has overcome the darkness.

My favorite example of final rewards from our fantasy stories is found at the end of *The Last Battle*. Tirian, Eustace and Jill are forced to enter the stable, expecting something dreadful, but as they pass through the stable door they enter Aslan's country, and they are changed. They are not like those just out of battle but "fresh and cool and clean" and dressed in fine clothes. There they meet with all the others who have previously entered Aslan's country, among them the great kings and queens of Narnia from the past, including Peter, Edmund and Lucy. Aslan observes that they do not look happy:

> Lucy said, "We're so afraid of being sent away, Aslan. And you have sent us back into our own world so often."
>
> "No fear of that," said Aslan. "Have you not guessed?"
>
> Their hearts leaped and a wild hope rose within them.
>
> "There *was* a real railway accident," said Aslan softly. "Your father and mother and all of you are—as you used to call it in the Shadow-Lands—dead. The term is over: the holidays have begun. The dream is ended: this is the morning."
>
> And as He spoke He no longer looked to them like a lion, but the things that began to happen to them after that were so great and beautiful that I cannot write them. And for us this is the end of all the stories, and we can most truly say that they all lived happily ever after. But for them, it was only the beginning of the real story. All their life in this world and all their adventures in Narnia had only been the cover and the title page: now at last they were beginning Chapter One of the Great Story, which no one on earth has read: which goes on forever: in which every chapter is better than the one before.

In the final chapter of the Bible, the risen and ascended Jesus says, "Behold, I am coming soon! My reward is with me, and I will give to everyone according to what he has done. I am the Alpha and the Omega, the First and the Last, the Beginning and the End" (Revelation 22:12). We who trust Jesus can trust that the Author of our story will finish it exquisitely.

TRANSFORMED

One further reward remains to be discussed. Over the course of their journey, those on the side of good have been transformed into heroes. The moment when they could truly be called heroes can't be pinpointed, but somewhere along the way—responding to the call, crossing over into the extraordinary, meeting with the mentor, sorting out their allies from their enemies, preparing for the coming ordeal, enduring tests, trials and tricksters, getting past threshold guardians—something happened within them. They came to know the true nature of evil and oppose it, they unveiled the shapeshifters, fought in the ultimate battle, combated the shadow of their dark nature, faced death, experienced grand rescues, resurrection and redemption, broke beyond the bounds of time, saw justice meted out and received their rewards. They were not overcome by evil but overcame evil with good. May we do likewise!

Epilogue

Return with the Elixir

"The stone will transform any metal into pure gold.
It also produces the Elixir of Life,
which will make the drinker immortal."

Harry Potter and the Sorcerer's Stone

The final stage of the hero's journey is to return with something of value to share with others to their benefit. This is commonly referred to as the "return with the elixir." Their adventure over, it's time for the heroes to return from their magical world to their home. Whatever adventures the hero has taken, whatever perils have been overcome, and whatever has been learned now needs to become of benefit to others as well.

At the end of *Star Wars: Return of the Jedi* the hero team returns bringing freedom from tyranny for their galaxy. Princess Leia and Han Solo return with love—which always tends to make the world a better place. Anakin Skywalker takes back his place as a Jedi Knight, making the final return to where he always belonged and bringing Luke reconciliation with his father and a source of spiritual support. As he takes his place alongside Obi-Wan Kenobi and Yoda, he brings with him love for his children, freedom from the oppressive grip of the Empire and, for us, the hope that even the worst of villains can change.

In *The Magician's Nephew* Digory returns from Narnia with healing fruit for his mother but also the seed that will grow into a point of entry into Narnia for others to follow in the future. He is fortunate enough to live to be an old man and counsel Peter, Susan, Edmund and Lucy to believe in other worlds, and to tell them that the wardrobe had magical properties. Passing on the possibility of adventure to another would-be hero is one of the best ways one can "return with the elixir."

In *Harry Potter and the Sorcerer's Stone* Harry literally returns with the elixir of life by coming back with the Sorcerer's Stone. Harry's fourth, fifth, and sixth years at Hogwarts end with Harry returning with his life—which is no small feat—but also with the realization that fighting evil is not a game. Professor Umbrage wanted dementors to suck out his soul; Voldemort wanted to kill him and use his blood to resurrect himself. While these may seem bleak, the elixir Harry returns with seems highly valuable for our world at this time in history: no matter the cost, we must recognize and oppose evil with all our strength and wisdom. As I write this we don't yet know how the final volume of *Harry Potter* will turn out, but I am confident we will see the hero team soundly defeat evil and return with a victory, with freedom preserved, the innocent protected and those on the side of good rewarded.

But what of us? I hope you have found something of value in this book you can take away with you to your benefit and of benefit to others. You may have learned something from the book or decided something in response to what you read here. The key in adventure stories, even our own, is to go through life's experiences looking for something of value we can pass on to others. I have a few suggestions.

The primary suggestion is that you take away a heightened realization of the power of stories, and that you would make a point of connecting with others around shared stories—stories you've enjoyed reading, personal stories and God's stories.

Hopefully you have thought more about what these stories teach us about navigating good and evil in the real world. I hope you will leave this book more determined to resist evil and take a stand with that which is good.

Look for opportunities to connect with people at points where the pop culture they enjoy reveals needs common to every human heart. These stories have the power to bring people together; in the introduction I mentioned how J. R. R. Tolkien (author of *The Lord of the Rings*) and C. S. Lewis (author of the Chronicles of Narnia) connected over literature and the meaning of myth. They drew closer to each other and eventually closer to God in that exploration. Each point of the hero's journey we looked at in this book touches the human heart and spirit in common ways. Therefore, we have many points where we can connect with other people as we exchange stories.

Consider how the hero's journey might be fulfilled in our life story as we appropriate and apply the truths we discover in the Bible.

- Might Jesus transform us so that we can sacrifice our lives for those we love? Might we call others to follow Jesus, assuring them that transformation takes place through the process, not before they start the journey?

- Might we share with others that there is more to life than the ordinary world they occupy, and encourage them to keep seeking until they cross the threshold into God's extraordinary kingdom?

- Might we share the good news that the Holy Spirit is here to be our mentor, to guide us and walk alongside us through life? Might we follow in the footsteps of faithful mentors and be a mentor to others?

- Might we build up our hero team by being a loyal ally to our friends? Might we seek out those within our reach who need a group where they can belong, and invite them in, offering support and love?

- Might we live a life in training, conducting ourselves with discipline, resisting evil and fighting to protect that which is good?

- When we see others struggling with tests, trials and challenges, might we encourage them not to give up? Might we share stories of how God has caused us to grow through our challenges, thus encouraging them to develop endurance, courage, perseverance and trust? Might we point them to the sacrifice of Jesus and the power of the Holy Spirit— the only way for any of us to win the ultimate battle against sin?

- Given that no one wants to be taken in by a shapeshifter, might we avoid hypocrisy and practice being trustworthy?

- Whenever someone we know is faced with the reality of death, might we offer hope for the quest for immortality built into our beings? Might we comfort them in their grief and assure them that God will finally defeat death?

- Might we seek to rescue others in need? Might we offer people hope by sharing stories of when God and other people came to our rescue? Might we keep believing in people—and praying fervently for them—until their redemption is complete?

- Might we do all we can to see our loved ones and communities safe, free and good?

- Might we look forward in confident hope that God is beyond the bounds of time, knows our past, present and future, loves us, and will lead us through in triumph if we follow him? Might we share this hope with others?

- Might we live in such a way that we will receive good rewards in the end—choosing that which is right over that which is easy, and encouraging others to turn from the dark path into God's kingdom?

- Might we share that which is of value with others to make the world a better place: kindness, mercy, help, financial resources, warmth, and the stories that connect us with the truth of God's love?

Live your adventure! Fight evil! Preserve that which is good! May God bless you in your journey and bless others through you!

Notes

Introduction

[1]Christopher Vogler, *The Writer's Journey* (Studio City, Calif.: Wiese, 1992), p. 26.

[2]C. S. Lewis, *Miracles* (New York: Macmillan, 1972), p. 139n.

[3]Thomas L. Martin, ed., *Reading the Classics with C. S. Lewis* (Grand Rapids: Baker Academic, 2000), p. 269.

[4]Ibid.

Chapter 1: "The Hero" and Would-Be Heroes Among Us

[1]William Herndon, *Herndon's Life of Lincoln* (New York: Da Capo Press, 1942), pp. 422-23.

Chapter 2: The Call to Join the Battle Against Evil

[1]Christopher Vogler, *The Writer's Journey* (Studio City, Calif.: Wiese, 1992), p. 71.

Chapter 3: Crossing the Threshold into the Extraordinary

[1]Walter Hooper, *C. S. Lewis Companion & Guide* (San Francisco: HarperSanFrancisco, 1996), p. 399.

[2]C. S. Lewis, "On Three Ways of Writing for Children," in *Of Other Worlds: Essays and Stories,* ed. Walter Hooper (New York: Harcourt, 1966), p. 27.

[3]Cath Filmer-Davies, "Fantasy," in *Reading the Classics with C. S. Lewis,* ed. Thomas L. Martin (Grand Rapids: Baker Academic, 2000), pp. 286-87.

[4]C. S. Lewis, "Sometimes Fairy Stories May Say Best What's to Be Said," in *Of Other Worlds: Essays and Stories,* ed. Walter Hooper (New York: Harcourt, 1966), p. 37.

[5]Those interested in such details can find a complete accounting in one of the Hogwarts School books *Fantastic Beasts and Where to Find Them by Newt Scamander.* It's published in our world by Arthur A. Levine Books, an imprint of Scholastic Inc. There are also excellent resources such as the *Fantasy Encyclopedia: A Guide to Fabulous Beasts and Magical Beings—from Elves to Dragons to Vampires and Wizards,* written by Judy Allen and beautifully illustrated by John Howe. Other resources specifically focus on the fantastic creatures in Harry Potter books, including *Fact, Fiction,*

and Folklore in Harry Potter's World: An Unofficial Guide by George Beahm. There are books chronicling fantastic creatures in Narnia too. My favorite is *Companion to Narnia: A Complete Guide to the Enchanting World of C. S. Lewis's "The Chronicles of Narnia"* by Paul F. Ford.

[6]Filmer-Davies, "Fantasy," p. 286.

Chapter 10: Fighting the Ultimate Battles

[1]C. S. Lewis, *Of Other Worlds: Essays and Stories,* ed. Walter Hooper (New York: Harcourt, 1994), p. 31. The Ogpu was the Russian secret police feared during the cold war at the time Lewis was writing.

[2]This is not to condemn anyone who has been divorced against their will or who has chosen divorce within scriptural allowances, nor even to condemn those Christians who have disobeyed God's word by divorcing without scriptural grounds. The evil one will attack every Christian marriage, and we must actively strengthen our marriage so that we don't see a good marriage lost.

Chapter 11: Combating the Shadow of our Own Dark Nature

[1]Christopher Vogler, *The Writer's Journey* (Studio City, Calif.: Wiese, 1992), p. 71.

Chapter 13: Grand Rescues, Resurrection and Redemption

[1]C. S. Lewis, *Mere Christianity* (New York: HarperCollins, 1952), p. 50.